Awakening Young Minds

This is a Malor Book
Published by ISHK

P. O. Box 381069, Cambridge, MA 02238-1069

©The Institute for the Study of Human Knowledge 1997.
Los Altos, California

Awakening young minds : perspectives on education / compiled by
Denise D. Nessel.
    p. cm.
  Includes bibliographical references.
  ISBN 1-883536-05-7
  1. Education—Philosophy. 2. Teaching. 3. Learning. 4. Schools.
I. Nessel, Denise D., 1943-
LB14.7.A93 1997
370'.1—dc20

                                        96-28684
                                             CIP

Contents

About the Compiler:

Denise Nessel, Ph.D., has worked as a teacher, a university professor, and a school-district supervisor of curriculum and instruction. She has co-authored four methods books for teachers and has designed and written a variety of print and electronic instructional materials for students. Denise currently resides in California and is a senior consultant with the National Urban Alliance for Effective Education (NUA), an education consortium based at Teachers College, Columbia University, whose members are dedicated to improving the way students think and learn.

INTRODUCTION

by Denise D. Nessel

Introduction

by Denise D. Nessel

In 1892, in a lecture to teachers, William James told of a friend who, when visiting a geography class, was invited to test the students' knowledge. The visitor, knowing what the class had been studying, asked: "Suppose you should dig a hole in the ground, hundreds of feet deep. How would you find it at the bottom—warmer or colder than on top?" When no one could answer, the teacher explained that the question needed to be worded differently, and she asked the class herself: "In what condition is the interior of the globe?" Immediately, the students piped: "The interior of the globe is in a condition of igneous fusion."

As many teachers discover, to their amusement and dismay, students today can achieve equally superficial states of understanding. Fortunately, most teachers are not satisfied with such responses and aim to get beyond them to true comprehension—real learning. To some, this means developing solid facility with reading, writing, and calculating while mastering the facts and concepts of the subject matter. Others include the ability to sustain interest and effort with studies in the absence of rewards or punishments. Still others argue that students have not really learned unless they have not only mastered basics and are self-motivated but also have developed inquiring minds and critical thinking abilities. Such teachers are not satisfied unless their students develop enough intellectual self-reliance to question sources of information and opinions, including their textbooks and teachers.

When the goal is to get beyond parroted statements to real learning—however that is defined—the task is not easy, and when students do not learn, or learn less than they might, the reasons are not always clear. Have the problems developed because of ineffective teaching methods? Inappropriate expectations? Apathetic parents? Disadvantaged backgrounds? Low motivation? Attention disorders? Boring materials? Too much discipline? Too little discipline? Irrelevant curricula? Large classes? Peer group pressure? Television? The answer, depending on the student, is: all, some, or none of the above. That is, the reasons students do not learn vary with the circumstances. The solution is thus not to impose on all a specific curriculum, method of instruction, or disciplinary program although it is tempting to look for such a quick fix or panacea.

A more fruitful approach is for those involved to give careful thought to what they are doing and why so that they may refine and improve their efforts. That goes for teachers, administrators, students, and others who participate in an educational enterprise. Of course, critical reflection sometimes reveals that one is contributing to a problem in the attempt to solve it or that one is moving rapidly in the wrong direction. But such discoveries, uncomfortable though they may be, can lead to improvements. Examining the situation thoughtfully can also reduce the tendency to blame difficulties on externals and conclude that nothing can be done. In fact, even the most discouraging externals can be overcome, eliminated, or transformed. For example, Jaime Escalante showed, to almost everyone's surprise, that his disadvantaged students could excel in calculus. Reuven Feuerstein achieved seeming miracles with children whom others considered hopelessly retarded. Paulo Freire helped dreadfully impoverished peasants learn to read and write, think critically, and take charge of their lives. These are only a few of the many teachers who have inspired students and colleagues by changing supposedly fixed realities. They did so by looking clearly at their situations, recognizing faulty assumptions, and using intelligence and skill to improve the conditions for learning.

For those who wish to give careful thought to the current conditions of education with an eye to improving them, the selections in this book may be helpful. They represent a range of perspectives on the institution of school and the processes of teaching and learning. Some were written many years ago and yet are as relevant as the ones that appeared in print quite recently, showing that teachers from one generation to the next have surprisingly similar concerns. In fact, a perennial challenge for educators is the one about which Plato wrote in *The Republic:* how to avoid simply feeding students information and instead get them to use their innate capacities and think for themselves. The former results in students who can spit back "the interior of the globe is in a condition of igneous fusion" without having any idea what that means. The latter, which requires considerable sensitivity and skill on the part of the teacher, leads to real learning.

EDUCATION
AND CULTURE

by Leo Tolstoy

From *Tolstoy on Education,* translated by Leo Wiener and introduced by Reginald D. Archambault (Chicago: University of Chicago Press, 1967, pages 143-151). Used by permission of the University of Chicago Press.

Leo Tolstoy was deeply dissatisfied with the process of education as he knew it. He explored different approaches to learning in the school for peasant children that he established on his estate in 1861. Shortly after that, he wrote this essay, in which he explains why he believes that schools, as institutions, actually interfere with education.

Education and Culture

by Leo Tolstoy

In order to answer the questions put to us, we will only transpose them: (1) What is meant by non-interference of the school in education? (2) Is such a non-interference possible? (3) What must the school be, if it is not to interfere in education?

To avoid misunderstandings, I must first explain what I mean by the word "school," which I used in the same sense in my first article. By the word "school" I understand not the house in which the instruction is given, not the teachers, not the pupils, not a certain tendency of instruction, but, in the general sense, *the conscious activity of him who gives culture upon those who receive it,* that is, one part of culture, in whatever way this activity may find its expression: the teaching of the regulations to a recruit is a school; public lectures are a school; a course in a Mohammedan institution of learning is a school; the collections of a museum and free access to them for those who wish to see them are a school.

I reply to the first question. The non-interference of the school in matters of culture means the non-interference of the school in the culture [formation] of beliefs, the convictions, and the character of him who receives that culture. This non-interference is obtained by granting the person under culture the full freedom to avail himself of the teaching which answers his need, which he wants, and to avail himself of it to the extent to which he needs and wants it, and to avoid the teaching which he does not need and which he does not want.

Public lectures, museums are the best examples of schools without interference in education. Universities are examples of schools with interference in matters of education. In these institutions the students are confined to certain limits by a definite course, a programme, a code of selected studies, by the exigencies of the examinations, and by the grant of rights, based chiefly on these examinations, or, more correctly, by the deprivation of rights in case of non-compliance with certain prescribed conditions. (A senior taking his examinations threatened with one of the most terrible punishments—with the loss of his ten or twelve years of labour in the gymnasium and in the university, and with the loss of all the advantages in view of which he bore privations for the period of twelve years.)

In these institutions everything is so arranged that the student, being threatened with punishments, is obliged in receiving his culture to adopt that educational element and to assimilate those beliefs, those convictions, and that character, which the founders of the institution want. The compulsory educational element, which consists in the exclusive choice of one circle of sciences and in the threat of punishment, is as strong and as patent to the serious observer, as in that other institution with corporal punishment, which superficial observers oppose to the universities.

Public lectures, whose number is on the continuous increase in Europe and in America, on the contrary, not only do not confine one to a certain circle of knowledge, not only do not demand attention under threat of punishment, but expect from the students certain sacrifices, by which they prove, in contradistinction to the first, the complete freedom of choice and of the basis on which they are reared. That is what is meant by interference and non-interference of school in education.

If I am told that such non-interference, which is possible for the higher institutions and for grown-up people, is not possible for the lower schools and for minors, because we have no example for it in the shape of public lectures for children, and so forth, I will answer that if we are not going to understand the word "school" in the narrowest sense, but will accept it with the above-mentioned definition, we shall find for the lower stages of knowledge and for the lower ages many influences of liberal culture without interference in education, corresponding to the higher institutions and to the public lectures. Such is the acquisition of the art of reading from a friend or a brother; such are popular games of children, of the cultural value of which we intend writing a special article; such are public spectacles, panoramas, and so forth; such are pictures and books; such are fairy-tales and songs; such are work and, last, the experiments of the school at Yásnaya Polyána.

The answer to the first question gives a partial answer to the second: is such a non-interference possible? We cannot prove this possibility theoretically. The one thing which confirms such a possibility is the observation which proves that people entirely uneducated, that is, who are subject only to the free cultural influences, the men of the people are fresher, more vigorous, more powerful, more independent, juster, humaner, and, above all, more useful than men no matter how educated. But it may be that even this statement need be proved to many.

I shall have to say a great deal about these proofs at a later time. Here I will adduce one fact. Why does the race of educated people not perfect itself zoologically? A race of thoroughbred animals keeps improving; the race of educated people grows worse and weaker. Take at haphazard one hundred children of several educated generations and one hundred uneducated children of the people, and compare them in anything you please: in strength, in agility, in mind, in the ability to acquire knowledge, even in morality—and in all respects you are startled by the vast superiority on the side of the children of uneducated generations, and this superiority will be the greater, the lower the age, and vice versa. It is terrible to say this, on account of the conclusions to which it leads us, but it is true. A final proof of the possibility of non-interference in the lower schools, for people, to whom personal experience and an inner feeling tell nothing in favour of such an opinion, can be obtained only by means of a conscientious study of all those free influences by means of which the masses get their culture, by an all-round discussion of the question, and by a long series of experiments and reports upon it.

What, then, must the school be if it is not to interfere in matters of education? A school is, as said above, the conscious activity of him who gives culture upon those who receive it. How is he to act in order not to transgress the limits of culture, that is, of freedom?

I reply: the school must have one aim—the transmission of information, of knowledge, without attempting to pass over into the moral territory of convictions, beliefs, and character; its aim is to be nothing but science, and not the results of its influence upon human personality. The school must not try to foresee the consequences produced by science, but, in transmitting it, must leave full freedom for its application. The school must not regard any one science, nor a whole code of sciences, as necessary, but must transmit that information which it possesses, leaving the students the right to acquire it or not.

The structure and the programme of the school must be based not on theoretical speculations, not on the conviction held in regard to the necessity of such and such sciences, but on the mere possibilities, that is, the knowledge of the teachers.

I will explain it by an example.

I want to establish an institution of learning. I form no programme which is based on my theoretical conceptions, and on the basis of this programme look about for teachers, but I propose to all people who feel that they are called to furnish information to lecture or teach such subjects as they know best. Of course, my former experience will guide me in the selection of these lessons, that is, we shall not try to offer subjects such as nobody wants to listen to,—in a Russian village we will not teach Spanish, or astrology, or geography, just as a merchant will not open shops of surgical instruments or of crinolines in this village.

We may foresee a demand for what we offer; but our final judge will be only experience, and we do not think we have the right to open a single shop, in which we are to sell tar with this condition, that to every ten pounds of tar every purchaser must buy a pound of ginger or of pomatum. We do not trouble ourselves about the use to which our wares will be put by the purchasers, believing that they know what they want, and that we have enough to do to discover their needs and to provide for them.

It is quite possible that there will turn up one teacher of zoology, one teacher of medieval history, one of religion, and one of the art of printing. If these teachers will know how to make their lessons interesting, these lessons will be useful, in spite of their seeming incompatibility and accidentalness. I do not believe in the possibility of a theoretically established, harmonious code of sciences, but that every science, being the subject of free instruction, harmonizes with all the others into one code of knowledge for each man.

I shall be told that in such an accidentalness of programme there may enter useless, even injurious, sciences into the course, and that many sciences could not be given because the students would not be sufficiently prepared for them.

To this I will reply that, in the first place, there are no injurious and no useless sciences for anybody, and that we have, as an assurance of that, the common sense and the needs of the students, who, the instruction being free, will not admit useless and injurious sciences, if there were such; that, in the second place, prepared pupils are wanted only for a poor teacher, but that for a good teacher it is easier to begin algebra or analytical geometry with a pupil who does not know arithmetic than with a pupil who knows it poorly, and that it is easier to lecture on medieval history to students who have not studied ancient history. I do not believe that a professor, who in a university lectures on differential and integral calculus, or on the history of the Russian civil law, and who cannot teach arithmetic, or Russian history in a primary school,—I do not believe that he can be a good professor. I see no use and no merit in good instruction in one part of a subject, and even no possibility of giving it. Above all, I am convinced that the supply will always correspond to the demand, and that at each stage of science there will be found a sufficient number of both students and teachers.

But how, I shall be told, can a person who teaches culture help wishing to produce a certain educational influence by means of his instruction? This tendency is most natural; it is a natural exigency in the transmission of knowledge from him who offers culture to him who receives it. This tendency only imparts strength to the instructor to occupy himself with his subject,—it gives him that degree of enthusiasm which is necessary for him. It is impossible to deny this tendency, and it has never occurred to me to deny it; its existence so much more cogently proves to me the necessity of freedom in the matter of instruction.

A man who loves and teaches history cannot be prohibited from endeavouring to impart to his students that historical conception which he himself possesses, which he regards as useful and absolutely necessary for a man's development; a teacher cannot be prohibited from imparting that method in the study of mathematics or natural science which he considers the best; on the contrary, this prevision of the educational purpose encourages the teacher. The thing is that the educational element of science shall not be imparted by compulsion. I cannot carefully enough direct the reader's attention to this circumstance.

The educational element, let us say in mathematics or in history, is only then imparted to the students when the teacher is passionately fond of his subject and when he knows it well; only then his love is communicated to the students and has an educational influence upon them. In the contrary case, that is, when it has been decided somewhere that such and such a subject has an educational value, and one is instructed to teach, and the others to listen to it, the teaching accomplishes the very opposite results, that is, it not only does not educate scientifically, but also makes the science loathsome.

It is said that science has in itself an educational element *(erziehliges Element);* that is true and not true, and in this very statement lies the fundamental error of the existing paradoxical view on education. Science is science and has nothing in itself. The educational element lies in the teaching, of the sciences, in the teacher's love for his science, and in the love with which it is imparted,—in the teacher's relation to his students. *If you wish to educate the student by science, love your science and know it, and the students will love both you and the science, and you will educate them; but if you yourself do not love it, the science will have no educational influence, no matter how much you may compel them to learn it.* Here again there is the one measure, the one salvation, the same freedom for the students to listen or not to listen to the teacher, to imbibe or not to imbibe his educational influence, that is, for them to decide whether he knows and loves his science.

Well, what, then, will the school be with the noninterference in education?

An all-sided and most varied conscious activity directed by one man on another, for the purpose of transmitting knowledge, without compelling the student by direct force or diplomatically to avail himself of that which we want him to avail himself of. The school will, perhaps, not be a school as we understand it,—with benches, blackboards, a teacher's or professor's platform—it may be a panorama, a theatre, a library, a museum, a conversation; the code of the sciences, the programme, will probably everywhere be different. (I know only my experiment: the school at Yásnaya Polyána, with its subdivision of subjects, which I have described, in the course of half a year completely changed, partly at the request of the pupils and their parents, partly on account of the insufficient information held by the teachers, and assumed other forms.)

What are we to do then? Shall there, really, be no county schools, no gymnasia, no chairs of the history of Roman law? "What will become of humanity?" I hear.

There certainly shall be none, if the pupils do not need them, and you are not able to make them good.

"But children do not always know what they need; children are mistaken," and so forth, I hear.

I will not enter into this discussion. This discussion would lead us to the question: Is man's nature right before the tribunal of man? and so forth. I do not know that it is, and do not take that stand; all I say is that if we can know what to teach, you must not keep me from teaching Russian children by force French, medieval genealogy, and the art of stealing. I can prove everything as you do.

"So there will be no gymnasia and no Latin? Then, what am I going to do?" I again hear.

Don't be afraid! There will be Latin and rhetoric, and they will exist another hundred years, simply because the medicine is bought, so we must drink it (as a patient said). I doubt whether the thought, which I have expressed, perhaps, indistinctly, awkwardly, inconclusively, will become the common possession in another hundred years; it is not likely that within a hundred years will die those ready-made institutions, schools, gymnasia, universities, and that within that time will grow up freely formed institutions, having for their basis the freedom of the learning generation.

INSTITUTIONAL CONSTRAINTS

by Howard Gardner

Schools as they exist today have resulted at least partly from society's attempts to educate larger and larger numbers of youngsters as efficiently as possible. Howard Gardner, distinguished Professor of Education at the Harvard Graduate School of Education, here discusses how these institutions have become barriers to the full development of learning capacity.

Please note that Gardner's remark about "the next chapter" in this selection is a reference to the next chapter of his book, not the next chapter of this volume.

Institutional Constraints

by Howard Gardner

I have argued that human beings are constrained by their species membership to learn in certain ways. Although schools harbor no genetic limitations, these institutions may also be thought of as peculiar kinds of organisms, with their own kinds of constraints. Some of these constraints probably characterize schools all over the world, while others prove specific to certain times, locales, and/or populations.

Beginning with those constraints that are likely to be encountered everywhere, schools are institutions that place together individuals who have not known one another, to work on tasks that appear more or less remote from the operation of the remainder of the society. It is therefore necessary to set up procedures by which the institution can run smoothly and to have rewards and punishments that are appropriate to its purposes. It is hardly ideal to have to transmit knowledge in mass form, with tens or scores of students in the same room, each with his own strengths and weaknesses, approaches to learning, goals, and aspirations. Teachers must also deal with noncognitive problems that beset their students, problems that are seemingly unrelated to the overt mission of schools yet that can cripple a class as effectively as would a plague or a fire.

Journalist Tracy Kidder has put it whimsically:

"The problem is fundamental. Put twenty or more children of roughly the same age in a little room, confine them to desks, make them wait in lines, make them behave. It is as if a secret committee, now lost to history, had made a study of children and, having figured out what the greatest number were least disposed to do, declared that all of them should do it."

The best teachers prove able to cope with these limitations, perhaps using some students to help others, presenting lessons that can speak to the range of students, or grouping students so that their nonacademic problems are less disruptive. But even these teachers are hindered in ways that a master or tutor working in a one-on-one situation would not be.

As institutions set apart from the rest of society, schools must confront their relation to their community. At various times and in various ways, schools have sought to build or maintain bridges with the family, the home, or other community institutions. For the most part, however, schools have found it more efficient to operate independently of other institutions. This practice proves particularly problematic in the contemporary society, where powerful educational (and noneducational) forces are constantly at work in the media, in the commercial sector, and on the streets. The decision to ignore these forces can be understood, and yet, precisely because they are so powerful and ubiquitous, these forces may well overwhelm the lessons and themes of school.

Just as the mind of the five-year-old endures in the school-age pupil, so too the values and practices of the wider community do not disappear just because the student happens to be sitting in class and listening to the teacher talk. Once the student departs from class at the end of the day, or at the end of her school career, the messages and practices featured on television, the objects prized by the consuming society, the games played in arcades or on the floor of the stock exchange achieve enormous salience. Just how to balance and integrate the mission of school with the practices of the wider community is a problem that few educational institutions have solved.

Schools are also bureaucratic institutions within communities and have additional constraints imposed by that factor. Inasmuch as schools always require support from the outside world, teachers and administrators must prove sensitive over the long run to the goals of those who pay for their operation. Particular goals will of course vary across communities and cultures. In modern Western industrialized society, extremes of bureaucratic constraints have been represented by France, on the one hand, and the United States, on the other. In the case of France, there is such tight control over the curriculum and syllabus that students all over the country (and in colonies and former colonies) study the same topics in the same way and are tested on them with the same examinations. Underlying the syllabi and the practices is the most important topic of all: a strong image of what it means to be an educated Frenchman or Frenchwoman. Interest in the annual baccalaureate examination is sufficiently high that the questions are published in the newspaper and reported on the television news. In the United States, by contrast, each of the more than fifteen thousand school districts has considerable autonomy over what is taught and how it is assessed. Talk of a national curriculum or a national examination system used to be out of the question, and even today such topics must be mentioned in very tentative terms.

Despite (or perhaps because of) local control, schools in the United States are subjected to many powerful pressures, from such bodies as teachers' and administrators' unions, school boards, state legislatures, and the voting public. (It should be noted that those in positions of most power often know little or nothing about the daily practices of education.) These combined pressures make it very difficult for individual teachers to operate with much autonomy or sense of empowerment. Perhaps as a reaction to the fact that external agencies so often attempt to institute far-reaching reforms "from the top," schools—like other bureaucratic institutions—have developed strong protective mechanisms that often preclude any meaningful kind of reform or strangle it before it has a chance to take hold.

Mechanisms mediating against change range from teachers' pressuring their peers not to work longer hours on an experimental program to the adoption of mandated textbooks that call for precisely the kind of fact-recollecting performances that educators are trying to reject. Paradoxically, if genuine change is actually to come about, it may be necessary *not* to impose change.

Even though educational systems may pay lip service to goals like "understanding" or "deep knowledge," they in fact prove inimical to the pursuit of these goals. Sometimes these goals are considered to be hopelessly idealistic or unrealistic; at most, in the view of educational bureaucrats, schools ought to produce citizens who exhibit some basic literacies and can hold a job. But even in cases where these goals are taken seriously, events conspire to undermine their pursuit. Particularly when systems are expected to produce hard evidence of their success, the focus sooner or later comes to fall on indices that are readily quantified, such as scores on objective tests. Measures of understanding must be postponed for another day or restricted to a few experimental schools, which are allowed to operate under waivers.

Educational researcher Linda McNeil has helped to elucidate the conflicts engendered by such a system. In the interests of efficiency and accountability school systems tend to mandate large sets of rules and procedures. Many of these have only questionable relevance to the daily operation of classes and to the learning of students, and yet all teachers and administrators must adhere to them. At the same time, teachers are often encouraged—at least at the rhetorical level—to take the initiative and to be forceful and imaginative in their teaching. In fact, however, they feel caught in a bind, for adhering to the regulations is so time-consuming and exhausting that little time or energy remains for innovation. Risking censure or worse, a few teachers will ignore the regulations in order to pursue a more individualized program of instruction. Most teachers, however, will achieve an uneasy truce, with both their superiors and their students, by adopting "defensive teaching." Adhering to the rules, not making excessive demands on anyone (including themselves), asking students mostly to memorize definitions and lists rather than to tackle challenging problems, they will maintain control over their classrooms, but at the cost of educational inspiration. As McNeil phrases it, "When the school's organization becomes centered on managing and controlling, teachers and students take school less seriously. They fall into a ritual of teaching and learning that tends toward minimal standards and minimum effort." In terminology on which I elaborate in the next chapter, schools everywhere have embraced "correct-answer compromises" instead of undertaking "risks for understanding."

Nearly all the problems and constraints routinely encountered in schools are exacerbated in the urban American schools of today. Problems are almost always magnified in large bureaucratic settings, where many thousands of teachers, administrators, and students must be "served" and the pressures for uniform treatment of diverse "customers" are profound. Classes are larger and more difficult to control; students are often unmotivated, and they may be frightened, agitated, hungry, or ill as well; regulations proliferate with little rhyme or reason. Teachers feel buffeted about by contradictory messages: Students should learn cooperatively, and yet a separate evaluation must be performed on each individual student; children with problems should be "mainstreamed," and yet it is important to track the talented students so that they can gain college admission; teachers are expected to act in a professional manner, and yet their every move is scrutinized by various monitoring bodies. The result is a virtual logjam in many of our nation's public schools.

Even when classes are small and students are motivated, it is necessary for teachers both to be truly knowledgeable and to know how to transmit the desired or required knowledge to students. In some societies, teachers are selected with great care, well trained by master teachers, ultimately given considerable autonomy, and encouraged to remain in the classroom rather than to assume administrative posts. Education—indeed, even education for understanding—can flourish under such circumstances. In most cases, however, school teaching, at least below the secondary or higher levels, is considered a low-prestige occupation, and those charged with the education of the young may have only modest intellectual abilities and pedagogical skills. The gifted women who might have gone (or perhaps would have been forced to go) into teaching two generations ago are now attracted to higher-paying, more prestigious positions, depriving the schools of a cohort that was of enormous value in the past.

As a final institutional feature, schools must be accountable for the progress of their students. To ensure that the education has been successful, it is important to be able to "debrief" students. In the past, because teachers often remained with the same students for several years and because the demands of the curricula were less burdensome, much of this assessment could be handled in the course of daily interchanges. Today, however, schools throughout the world have moved toward less personalized forms of assessment. Certain economic and meritocratic advantages are associated with the adoption of standardized instruments and with regular calculations of "seat time," "time on task," and dropout and promotion rates. Yet the kinds of instruments increasingly favored often prove remote from the deeper kinds of understanding that many educators would like students to acquire.

Because of such pervasive constraints on human learning and a parallel set of constraints operating on community institutions, it is difficult to mount an effective school and even more difficult to demonstrate that it has been effective. We run the risk of investing incalculable resources in institutions that do not operate very well and that may never approach the effectiveness that their supporters—and, for that matter their detractors—would desire. Moreover, it is my own belief that until now, we have not fully appreciated just how difficult it is for schools to succeed in their chosen (or appointed) task. Reflecting the argument of this book, we have not been cognizant of the ways in which basic inclinations of human learning turn out to be ill-matched to the agenda of the modern secular school.

THE NINE MYTHS
OF SCHOOLING

by John Taylor Gatto

From *Liberty* Vol. 9, No. 1 (September 1995), pages 31-34. Copyright © 1995 by John Taylor Gatto. Used by permission of John Taylor Gatto and the editors of *Liberty*, P. O. Box 1181, Port Townsend, WA 98368.

John Taylor Gatto here questions certain basic assumptions on which the American public school system is based and makes some interesting comparisons between U.S. schools and schools abroad. His thought-provoking observations stem from the high value he places on individual liberty as a worthy goal of a free society.

The Nine Myths of Schooling

by John Taylor Gatto

The Swiss, just like us, believe that education is the key to their national success. But that's where the similarity ends. In 1990, about 50% of American secondary-school graduates enrolled in college, but only 22% did in Switzerland. In America, almost 100% of our kids go to high school or private equivalents, but under a quarter of Swiss kids do. And yet the Swiss per-capita income is the highest of any nation in the world, and the Swiss keep insisting that virtually everyone in their country is highly educated!

Remember, we're talking about a sophisticated economy that produces the highest per-capita paycheck in the world. High for the lightly schooled as well as the heavily schooled. Higher than Japan's, Germany's, or our own. What on Earth could be going on?

No one goes to high school in Switzerland who doesn't also want to go to college; three-quarters of the young people enter apprenticeships instead. It seems the Swiss don't make the mistake that schooling and education are synonyms.

If you are thinking silently at this point that apprenticeships as a substitute for classroom confinement isn't a very shocking idea—and that it has the drawback of locking kids away from later choosing white-collar work—think again. I wasn't talking about blue-collar apprenticeships (though the Swiss have those, too) but white-collar apprenticeships in abundance. Many top managers of Swiss insurance companies, manufacturing firms, and banks never saw the inside of a high school, let alone a college.

Well, *shocking* is the word for it, isn't it? I mean, here you are putting away your loot in a Swiss bank because it's safe over there and not so safe here, and now I've told you the bank president may only have a sixth-grade education. Just like Shakespeare.

As long as we're playing "Did you know?"—did you know that in Sweden, a country legendary for its quality of life, a nation that outperforms America in every academic category, kids aren't allowed to start school before age seven? The hard-headed Swedes don't want to pay for the social pathologies attendant on ripping a child away from his home and mother and dumping him into a pen with strangers. Can you remember the last time you worried about a Swedish Volvo breaking down prematurely or a Swedish jet engine failing in the air?

Did you know that the entire Swedish school sequence is only nine years long, a net 25% time and tax savings over our own twelve-year sequence?

Did you know that students in Hong Kong, a country with a population the size of Norway's, beat Japanese students in every scientific and mathematical category? Did you know that Hong Kong has a school year ten weeks shorter than Japan's? How on Earth do they manage that if longer school years translate into higher performance?

Why do you suppose you haven't heard about Hong Kong? You've heard enough about Japan, I'm sure.

But I'll bet you haven't heard that in Japan, a recess is held after every class period.

Or that in Flemish Belgium, the country with the shortest school year in the developed world, the kids regularly finish in the top three nations in international academic competition. Is it the water in Belgium or what? Their success obviously didn't come from any passionate commitment to forced schooling.

Did you know that three British prime ministers in this century, including the current one, didn't bother to go to college?

Exactly in whose interest do you think it is that the *New York Times*—and just about every other outlet for American journalism—doesn't make information like this readily accessible?

If you trust journalists or the professional educational establishment to provide you with the data you need to think for yourself about schooling, you're the kind of citizen who would trade his cow for a handful of colored beans.

Why School?

Shortly into the twentieth century, American educators decided to move away from justifying their jobs with the rhetoric of intellectual development and skills training, and to enter the eerie world of social engineering, a world where "socializing" and "psychologizing" the classroom preempts attention and rewards. Professionalization of the administrative/teaching staff was an important preliminary mechanism to this end, serving as a sieve to remove troublesome interlopers and providing lucrative rewards for allies and camp followers.

Non-intellectual, non-skill schooling was supported by a strange and motley collection of fellow travelers: by unions, yes, but also by such legendary businessmen as Carnegie and Rockefeller, Ford and Astor; by genuine ideologues like John Dewey, yes, but many academic opportunists as well, such as Nicholas Murray Butler of Columbia. Prominent colleges such as Johns Hopkins and Chicago played a large part in the deconstruction of American academic schooling, as did a powerful core of private foundations and think tanks.

Whether they did this out of conviction, for private advantage, or any hybrid of these reasons and more I'll leave for others to debate. What is certain is that the outcome aimed for—socializing children into creatures who would no longer feel easy with their own parents, psychologizing children into dependable and dependent camp followers—had little to do with why parents thought children were ordered into schools.

In the early years of this century, a radical shift was underway, transforming a society of farmers, craftspeople, fishermen, and small entrepreneurs into the disciplined workforce of a corporate state, one in which all the work is sucked into colossal governments, colossal institutions, and colossal business enterprises—a society whose driving logic is comfort, security, predictability, and consensus rather than independence, originality, risk-taking, and uncompromising principle. In the gospel of social engineering this transformation was to lead to a future utopia of welfare capitalism. With the "problem of production" solved, the attention of professional intellectuals and powerful men of wealth turned to controlling distribution, so that a "rational" society, defined as a stable state without internal or external conflicts, could be managed for nations, regions, and eventually the entire planet. In such a system, if you behave, you get a share of the divvy; if you don't, your share is correspondingly reduced. Keep in mind that a small farmer, a carpenter, a fisherman, a seamstress, or an Indian fighter never gave undue attention to being well-behaved and you will begin to see how a centralized economy and centralized schooling box human behavior into a much narrower container than it normally would occupy. You will begin to see why intellectual development, for all its theoretical desirability, can never really be a serious goal for a society seeking comfort, security, predictability, and consensus; indeed, that such a fate must be actively avoided.

Once this design was in place—and it was firmly in place by 1917—all that remained to reach the target was a continual series of experiments on public schoolchildren: some modest in scope; many breathtakingly radical, such as "IQ tests" and "kindergartens"; and a full palette of intermediate colors, from "multiculturalism" to "rainbow" curricula to "universal self-esteem."

Each of these thrusts has a part to play in the movement toward the larger planners' utopia. Yet each is capable of being rhetorically defended as the particular redress of some current problem.

The biggest obstacle to a planned society is parents. Parents have their own plans for their own children. Most love their kids, so their motivations are self-reinforcing, unlike those of schoolpeople who "work with children" for a paycheck. Unless held in check, even a few unhappy parents can disrupt the conduct of an educational experiment. The second biggest obstacle to a planned society is religious sects, each of which maintains that God has a plan for all human beings, including children. And the third biggest obstacle is local values and ethnic cultures, which also provide alternative maps for growing up. Each of these three is an external force bidding against the school system for children's loyalties.

One final obstacle—a colossal one—is the individual nature of each particular child. John Locke pulled a whopper when he maintained that children are blank slates waiting to be written upon. He should have asked a few mothers about that. If you watch children closely under controlled conditions, as I did for 30 years as a schoolteacher, you can hardly fail to conclude that each kid has a private destiny he or she is pulled towards wordlessly—a destiny frequently put out of reach by schoolteachers, school executives, and project officers from the Ford Foundation.

In a planned society, individuality, cultural identity, a relationship with God, and close-knit families must be suppressed, if not totally extinguished. The Soviet Union was an object lesson in this utopian undertaking; the United States has gone down the same road, albeit with more hesitations, at least since the end of the First World War. If the social engineers are to accomplish such a complex transformation of nature into mechanism, the general public must be led to agree to certain apparently sensible assumptions—such as the assumption that a college degree is necessary for a high-status career, even though Swiss corporations and the British government are often run by managers without college training.

The security of schooling depends on many such assumptions, some of which, by adroit concealments worthy of a card sharp, seem to link schooling and future responsibility; and some of which serve to exalt the political state, diminish essential human institutions like the family, or define human nature as mean, violent, and brutish. I'd like to list nine specimens of these assumptions for you, to allow you to gauge which ones you personally accept, and to what degree.

Nine Assumptions

(1) Social cohesion is not possible through means other than government schooling. School is the main defense against social chaos.

(2) Children cannot learn to tolerate each other unless first socialized by government agents.

(3) The only safe mentors of children are certified experts with government-approved conditioning; children must be protected from the uncertified, including parents.

(4) Compelling children to violate family, cultural, and religious norms does not interfere with the development of their intellects or characters.

(5) In order to dilute parental influence, children must be disabused of the notion that mother and father are sovereign in morality or intelligence.

(6) Families should be encouraged to expend concern on the general education of everyone but discouraged from being unduly concerned with their own children's education.

(7) The state has predominant responsibility for training, morals, and beliefs. Children who escape state scrutiny will become immoral.

(8) Children from families with different beliefs, backgrounds, and styles must be forced together even if those beliefs violently contradict one another. Robert Frost was wrong when he maintained that "good fences make good neighbors."

(9) Government coercion can serve the cause of liberty.

Twenty-One Facts

These assumptions and a few others associated with them lead directly to the shape, style, and exercise of contemporary school politics. And these primary assumptions generate secondary assumptions that fuel the largely phony school debate played out in American journalism, a debate where the most important questions are never asked.

I once had dinner at the same table as Fred Hechinger, education editor of the *New York Times*. When I raised the possibility that the *Times* framed its coverage to omit inconvenient aspects of school questions (such as challenging the presumed connection between quantity of money spent on schools and quality of education), Mr. Hechinger became very angry and contemptuously dismissed my contention. Almost the same thing happened on a different occasion, when I dined at the same table as Albert Shanker of the American Federation of Teachers.

With that history of failure in opening a dialogue with some of the powers and principalities of institutional education—and I could add Lamar Alexander, Bill Bennett, Joe Fernandez, Diane Ravitch, Chester Finn, and many others to the list of luminaries who have listened to me only with impatience—I've turned to addressing the general public instead. I have tried to refute the assumptions schools rely on by drawing people's attention to several facts open to formal verification (or the informal variety grounded in common sense):

(1) There is no relationship between the amount of money spent on schooling and "good" results as measured by parents of any culture. This seems to be because "education" is not a commodity to be purchased but an enlargement of insight, power, understanding, and self-control almost completely outside the cash economy. Education is overwhelmingly an internally generated effort. The five American states that usually spend the least per capita on schooling are the five that usually have the best test results (although Iowa, which is about thirtieth in spending, sometimes creeps into the honored circle).

(2) There is no compelling evidence showing a positive relationship between length of schooling and

accomplishment. Many countries with short school years outperform those with long ones by a wide margin.

(3) Most relationships between test scores and job performance are illegitimate, arranged in advance by only allowing those testing well access to work. Would you hire a newspaper reporter because he had A's in English? Have you ever asked your surgeon what grade he got in meat-cutting? George Kennan, intellectual darling of the Washington elite some while ago—and the author of our containment policy against the Soviet Union—often found his secondary-school math and science grades below 60, and at Princeton he had many flunks, D's, and C's. "Sometimes," he said, "it is the unadjusted student struggling to forge his own standards who develops within himself the thoughtfulness to comprehend." Dean Acheson, Harry Truman's secretary of state, graduated from Groton with a 68 average. The headmaster wrote to his mother, "He is ... by no means a pleasant boy to teach." Einstein, we all know, was considered a high-grade moron, as were Thomas Edison and Benjamin Franklin. Is there anybody out there who really believes that grades and test scores are the mark of the man?

(4) Training done on the job is invariably cheaper, quicker, and of much higher quality than training done in a school setting.

If you wonder why that should be, consider that education and training are two different things, one residing largely in the development of good habits, the other in the development of vision, understanding, judgment, and the like. Education is self-training; it calls into its calculations mountains of personal data and experience that are simply unobtainable by any schoolteacher or higher pedagogue.

(5) In spite of relentless propaganda to the contrary, the American economy is tending to require *less* knowledge and *less* intellectual ability of its employees, not more. Scientists and mathematicians currently exist in numbers far exceeding any global or national demand—a condition that should grow much worse over the next decade, thanks to the endless hype of pedagogues and politicians. Schools could be restructured to teach children to develop intellect, resourcefulness, and independence, but that would lead in short order to structural changes in the old economy so profound that such a transformation is not likely to be allowed to happen.

(6) The habits, drills, and routines of government schooling sharply reduce initiative and creativity. Furthermore, the mechanism of why this is so has been well-understood for centuries.

(7) Teachers are paid as specialists but they almost never have any real-world experience in their specialties. Indeed, the low quality of their training has been a scandal for 50 years.

(8) A substantial amount of testimony exists from such highly regarded scientists as Richard Feynman, Albert Einstein, and many others that scientific discovery is negatively related to the procedures of school science classes.

(9) According to research by sociologist Christopher Jencks and others, the quality of the school any student attends is a very bad predictor of later success—financial, social, or emotional. On the other hand, quality of family life is a very good predictor.

(10) Children learn fastest and easiest when very young. General intelligence has usually developed as far as it will by the age of four. Most children are capable of reading and enjoying difficult material by that age and also capable of performing all the mathematical operations skillfully and with pleasure. Whether or not kids should do these things is a matter of philosophy and cultural tradition, not a course dictated by any scientific knowledge about the advisability of the practice.

(11) There is a direct relationship between heavy doses of teaching and detachment from reality. Many students so oppressed lose their links with past and future. And the bond with "now" is substantially weakened.

(12) Unknown to the public, virtually all famous remedial programs have failed. Such programs as Title I/Chapter 1 survive by the good will of political allies, not by results.

(13) There is no credible evidence that forced integration has any positive effect on student performance, but a large body of data suggests that the confinement of children from subcultures with children of a dominant culture does harm to the socially weaker group.

(14) Forced busing has accelerated the disintegration of minority neighborhoods without any visible academic benefit.

(15) There is no reason to believe that any existing educational technology can significantly improve intellectual performance. On the contrary, to the extent that machines establish the goals and work schedules, ask the questions, and monitor the performances, the already catastrophic

passivity and indifference created by forced confinement in school only increases.

(16) There is no body of knowledge inaccessible to a motivated elementary student. The sequences of development we use are hardly the product of "science"; they are legacies of unstable men like Pestalozzi and Froebel, and the military government of nineteenth-century Prussia from which we imported them.

(17) Delinquent behavior is a direct reaction to the structure of schooling. It is much worse than the press has reported because all urban school districts conspire to suppress its prevalence. Teachers who insist on justice on behalf of pupils and parents are most frequently intimidated into silence. Or dismissed.

(18) The rituals of schooling reduce mental flexibility, that characteristic vital for adjusting to different situations. Schools strive for uniformity in a world increasingly less uniform.

(19) Teacher-training courses are held in contempt by most practicing teachers as well as the general public, because expensive research has consistently failed to provide guidance to best practice.

(20) Schools create and maintain a caste system, separating children according to irrelevant parameters—poor, working-class, middle-class, and upper-middle-class kids are constantly made aware of alleged differences among themselves.

(21) Efforts to draw a child out of his culture or background has an immediate negative effect on his family relationships, his friendships, and the stability of his self-image.

A Closing Thought

There you have them: nine false assumptions and 21 assertions I think can be documented well enough to call facts. What can we do to remedy the problems that government schooling has caused? After spending 35 years in and around the institution (53 if I count my own time as inmate), the only way I can see to improve American education is to put full choice back into the hands of parents, let the marketplace redefine schooling—a job the special interests are incapable of—and encourage the development of as many styles of schooling as there are human dreams.

Let people, not bureaucrats, determine their own destinies.

INVITATION TO THE PAIN OF LEARNING

by Mortimer Adler

From *Reforming Education: The Opening of the American Mind* by Mortimer Adler, edited by Geraldine Van Doren (New York: Collier Books, Macmillan Publishing Company, 1990, pages 232-36). Used by permission of Macmillan/Simon & Schuster.

Critics of education have for many years made similar complaints: teachers are too soft, standards are too low, and children aren't learning nearly what they should. Such complaints are usually followed by a plea to return to the good old days—the days when the critic was in school. In this essay, Mortimer Adler also laments conditions, but he is interested in taking students far beyond the territory he may have covered as a pupil. First published in 1941, this essay is perhaps even more thought-provoking today, when the idea of "edutainment" is capturing many people's imaginations.

Invitation to the Pain
of Learning

by Mortimer Adler

One of the reasons why the education given by our
schools is so frothy and vapid is that the American people
generally—the parent even more than the teacher—wish
childhood to be unspoiled by pain. Childhood must be a
period of delight, of gay indulgence in impulses. It must
be given every avenue for unimpeded expression, which
of course is pleasant; and it must not be made to suffer
the impositions of discipline or the exactions of duty,
which of course are painful. Childhood must be filled with
as much play and as little work as possible. What cannot
be accomplished educationally through elaborate schemes
devised to make learning an exciting game must, of necessity, be forgone. Heaven forbid that learning should
ever take on the character of a serious occupation—just
as serious as earning money, and perhaps, much more la-
borious and painful.

The kindergarten spirit of playing at education pervades
our colleges. Most college students get their first taste of
studying as really hard work, requiring mental strain and
continual labor, only when they enter law school or medical school. Those who do not enter the professions find

out what working at anything really means only when they start to earn a living—that is, if four years of college has not softened them to the point which makes them unemployable. But even those who somehow recover from a college loaf and accept the responsibilities and obligations involved in earning a living—even those who may gradually come to realize the connection between work, pain, and earning—seldom if ever make a similar connection of pain and work with learning. "Learning" is what they did in college, and they know that that had very little to do with pain and work.

Now the attitude of the various agencies of adult education is even more softminded—not just softhearted—about the large public they face, a public which has had all sorts and amounts of schooling. The trouble is not simply that this large public has been spoiled by whatever schooling it has had—spoiled in the double sense that it is unprepared to carry on its own self-education in adult life and that it is disinclined to suffer pains for the sake of learning. The trouble also lies in the fact that agencies of adult education baby the public even more than the schools coddle the children. They have turned the whole nation—so far as education is concerned—into a kindergarten. It must all be fun. It must all be entertaining. Adult learning must be made as effortless as possible—painless, devoid of oppressive burdens and of irksome tasks. Adult men and women, because they are adult, can be expected to suffer pains of all sorts in the course of their daily occupations, whether domestic or commercial. We do not try to deny the fact that taking care of a household or holding down a job is necessarily burdensome, but we somehow still believe that the goods to be obtained, the worldly goods of wealth and comfort, are worth the effort. In any case, we know they cannot be obtained without effort. But we try to shut our eyes to the fact that improving one's mind or enlarging one's spirit is, if anything, more difficult than solving the problem of subsistence; or, maybe, we just do not believe that knowledge and wisdom are worth the effort.

We try to make adult education as exciting as a football game, as relaxing as a motion picture, and as easy on the mind as a quiz program. Otherwise, we will not be able to draw the big crowds, and the important thing is to draw large numbers of people into this educational game, even if after we get them there we leave them untransformed.

What lies behind my remark is a distinction between two views of education. In one view, education is something externally added to a person, as his clothing and other accoutrements. We cajole him into standing there willingly while we fit him; and in doing this we must be guided by his likes and dislikes, by his own notion of what enhances his appearance. In the other view, education is an interior transformation of a person's mind and character. He is plastic material to be improved not according to his inclinations, but according to what is good for him. But because he is a living thing and not dead clay, the transformation can be effected only through his own activity. Teachers of every sort can help, but they can only help in the process of learning that must be dominated at every moment by the activity of the learner. And the fundamental activity that is involved in every kind of genuine learning is intellectual activity, the activity generally known as thinking. Any learning which takes place without thinking is necessarily of the sort I have called external and additive—learning passively acquired, for which the common name is "information." Without thinking, the kind of learning which transforms a mind, gives it new insights, enlightens it, deepens understanding, elevates the spirit simply cannot occur.

Anyone who has done any thinking, even a little bit, knows that it is painful. It is hard work—in fact the very hardest that human beings are ever called upon to do. It is fatiguing, not refreshing. If allowed to follow the path of least resistance, no one would ever think. To make boys and girls, or men and women, think—and through thinking really undergo the transformation of learning—educational agencies of every sort must work against the grain, not with it. Far from trying to make the whole process painless from beginning to end, we must promise them the pleasure of achievement as a reward to be reached only through travail. I am not here concerned with the oratory that may have to be employed to persuade Americans that wisdom is a greater good than wealth, and hence worthy of greater effort. I am only insisting that there is no royal road, and that our present educational policies, in adult education especially, are fraudulent. We are pretending to give them something which is described in the advertising as very valuable, but which we promise they can get at almost no expense to them.

Not only must we honestly announce that pain and work are the irremovable and irreducible accompaniments of genuine learning, not only must we leave entertainment to the entertainers and make education a task and not a game, but we must have no fears about what is "over the public's head." Whoever passes by what is over his head condemns his head to its present low altitude; for nothing can elevate a mind except what is over its head; and that elevation is not accomplished by capillary attraction, but only by the hard work of climbing up the ropes, with sore hands and aching muscles. The school system which caters to the median child, or worse, to the lower half of the class; the lecturer before adults—and they are legion— who talks down to his audience; the radio or television program which tries to hit the lowest common denominator of popular receptivity—all these defeat the prime purpose of education by taking people as they are and leaving them just there.

The best adult education program that has ever existed in this country was one which endured for a short time under the auspices of the People's Institute in New York, when Everett Dean Martin was its director, and Scott Buchanan his assistant. It had two parts: one consisted of lectures which, so far as possible, were always aimed over the heads of the audience; the other consisted of seminars in which adults were helped in the reading of great books—the books that are over everyone's head. The latter part of the program is still being carried on by the staff of St. John's College in the cities near Annapolis; and we are conducting four such groups in the downtown college of the University of Chicago. I say that this is the only adult education that is genuinely educative simply because it is the only kind that requires activity, makes no pretense about avoiding pain and work, and is always working with materials well over everybody's head.

I do not know whether radio or television will ever be able to do anything genuinely educative. I am sure it serves the public in two ways: by giving them amusement and by giving them information. It may even, as in the case of its very best "educational" programs, stimulate some persons to do something about their minds by pursuing knowledge and wisdom in the only way possible—the hard way. But what I do not know is whether it can ever do what the best teachers have always done and must now be doing, namely, to present programs which are genuinely educative, as opposed to merely stimulating, in the sense that following them requires the listener to be active not passive, to think rather than remember, and to suffer all the pains of lifting himself up by his own bootstraps. Certainly so long as the so-called educational directors of our leading networks continue to operate on their present false principles, we can expect nothing. So long as they confuse education and entertainment, so long as they suppose that learning can be accomplished without pain, so long as they persist in bringing everything and everybody down to the lowest level on which the largest audience can be reached, the educational programs offered on the air will remain what they are today—shams and delusions.

It may be, of course, that the radio and television, for economic reasons must, like the motion picture, reach with certainty so large an audience that the networks cannot afford even to experiment with programs which make no pretense to be more palatable and pleasurable than real education can be. It may be that the radio and television cannot be expected to take a sounder view of education and to undertake more substantial programs than now prevail among the country's official leaders in education—the heads of our school system, of our colleges, of our adult education associations. But, in either case, let us not fool ourselves about what we are doing. "Education" all wrapped up in attractive tissue is the gold brick that is being sold in America today on every street corner. Everyone is selling it, everyone is buying it, but no one is giving or getting the real thing because the real thing is always hard to give or get. Yet the real thing can be made generally available if the obstacles to its distribution are honestly recognized. Unless we acknowledge that every invitation to learning can promise pleasure only as the result of pain, can offer achievement only at the expense of work, all of our invitations to learning, in school and out, whether by books, lectures, or radio and television programs will be as much buncombe as the worst patent medicine advertising, or the campaign pledge to put two chickens in every pot.

WHAT IS ABSOLUTE?

by Earl C. Kelley

From *Education for What is Real* by Earl C. Kelley (New York: Harper & Bros., 1947, pages 58-72). Copyright © 1947 by Earl C. Kelley, renewed © 1975 by Kate Winifred Gilmore. Reprinted by permission of HarperCollins Publishers, Inc.

While he was a professor of secondary education at Wayne State University, Earl Kelley visited the Hanover Institute in Hanover, New Hampshire, where Adelbert Ames, Jr., was investigating perception. Ames's demonstrations showed Kelley that what he had taken to be a fixed external reality was, instead, his own interpretation of sensory data. This insight forced him to examine some of his most basic assumptions and led directly to the writing of **Education for What is Real**. *In the preface to the book, he wrote that he believed "if we really master these basic facts of perception, they will tell us how to arrange for the growth of children, and from this point of departure we can finally establish what we may believe about teaching and learning." Almost fifty years later, information about the basic facts of perception is more widespread but has not really been mastered and applied within the profession of education or, for that matter, within society at large. For this reason, Kelley's observations are as relevant now as they were when his book was first published.*

Please note that Kelley's remarks about "Chapter III" and "Chapter IV" in this selection are references to chapters of his book, not chapters of this volume.

What Is Absolute?

by Earl C. Kelley

The demonstrations tell us some interesting things about the nature of knowledge. Since all we ever get of what is outside us is a prognosis, what we know becomes an entirely personal matter. I can get my stimuli from the same objects as you do, but I cannot bring the same purpose and experience to them that you do. Therefore they are never the same to you as they are to me. We cannot eliminate the viewing person, else nothing would happen at all. Further, it cannot be the same to me tomorrow as it is today, because tomorrow my whole experiencing make-up will be somewhat different.

We can therefore set out things to be learned, but we can never get the same learning twice, and the knowledge (what we know) resulting will vary among individuals and from time to time.

This is destructive of the idea that knowledge is absolute. We have long taught school as though it were, and we cling to the idea of absolutes because we think it gives us surety.

Our absolutes in the world of knowledge become a little ridiculous when we look back at the absolutes held by others in the past. We assume that they did not have the answers, but that we have. We laugh now at the "know-it-alls" who said the world was flat; we are mildly amused at those who found all the answers in Newtonian physics or in Euclidean mathematics. We find it easy to believe that while their answers were wrong, ours are correct; not only that they are correct, but that they include all there is to know. The "know-it-alls" in the future will laugh at our conceit.

Perhaps the mistake of regarding knowledge as an absolute, and as existing before learning can begin, is best illustrated by our teaching of history. Surely there is nothing more uncertain than facts as to what happened yesterday, to say nothing of a hundred years ago. In some of our classes, notably law and psychology, we stage incidents and ask students to write what they see, and then laugh at the wide disparity of the reports. But in history we take an account of an event which has been retold many times and teach it as truth. We are undisturbed by the fact that American History is one thing south of the Mason-Dixon line, another north of it, and still another in Canada. Equally good examples can be extracted from each of our several subjects. I was raised on Longfellow, but know little of Whitman. That is doubtless because my English teachers knew or liked Longfellow better than Whitman. But others, especially among our younger generation, know Whitman better than Longfellow. They doubtless will meet life quite as well as I, in spite of the fact that in my youth, knowledge of Longfellow was an absolute.

Since all I get is a prognosis, knowledge can never be absolute. It is what I extract from a situation when my experience and purpose are brought to bear on what comes to me from my environment, and from which I make my prognosis. It is personal, and different from any other knowing. It is the only kind of knowing (mine and not yours) which will serve my purpose.

The knowing that will serve me best is that which I seek out of a welter of infinite possibilities. Rather than take what has served another, which he offers for my service, I will do better if I seek out my own. Maybe if I had sought out the poetry that I could use best, I would be long on Whitman, short on Longfellow. To "acquire and accept" what is given to me by someone else implies the acquisition and acceptance of what someone else thinks is good for me.

Must We Depend on Absolutes for Surety?

Earlier, it has been mentioned that we like to believe in absolutes because they add to our sense of surety. More than that, we are accustomed to believe in them because most of us think the objects outside of us have meaning in themselves, whereas it has been shown that they only attain significance as we take account of them, and then they attain the significance which we assign to them. If we see that they have no meaning in themselves, but attain meaning in the light of each experiencing organism, then we see that they cannot be absolute.

To satisfy his need for surety, man is apt to assume that the things around him can be depended upon, and are therefore absolute. This probably comes from the fact that his prognosis of his surroundings in many instances is quite accurate. When he recognizes that what he gets from the things around him are only prognostic, and that those things therefore cannot be absolute, he pushes his absolutes further and further into the abstract world, until finally he settles for such abstractions as Truth, Freedom or Justice. But all these concepts are relative and related to a particular time and culture. From what we know of perception and reality, and the subjective, personal nature of these phenomena, about the only dependable fact is that whatever tomorrow will be, it will be different. New order is continually springing into form, and deteriorating into disorder. Schroedinger* points out that the atomic arrangements of the gene is the most persistent and permanent phenomenon in nature, but it is never the same in two individuals. When nature provides that the new individual shall come from two others, she provides for a sort of permanence, but also for change.

We Are Certain of Change

If we look upon life as a flowing and becoming process, implied from the nature of perception and reality, that the present is a momentary springboard for more becoming, then the fact of change becomes increasingly important. It really becomes something which we can accept as a constant. The most successful and adjusted people then will be those who know that whatever tomorrow may be, it must be different from today or yesterday, and who are ready, know how, and have assurance to meet tomorrow on that basis. They will not be filled with anxiety about tomorrow because they will have confidence and courage with which to meet it. They are the forward-looking people, as against the ones with eyes on the past, clinging to some sort of material or abstract absolute.

What About Authorities?

These ideas make trouble for those who would pose as authorities. It is true that one person can know more about some item than others. He can never know all about it, but he has selected one thing and has worked to improve his prognosis of it. Sometimes we say he knows more and more about less and less. But you and I can never get into his exact place, and we can never really make a fact ours completely because he says it is so. When we take it and fit it into our background, we take only the parts which we can make fit. It is then ours uniquely, and no longer his. We can of course learn from others, but we can only learn those parts of what others can offer which we can fit into *our* experience and purpose.

This makes the teacher's role as an authority untenable. In fact, he makes endless unnecessary trouble for himself in assuming this role. For what he can ever know about his subject is certain to be incomplete and tentative. If he is under the burden of making his students believe he is an authority, he has to delimit what his students can learn to what he knows. I once was a member of a class in botany, where the professor planned to take the class out to study all of the plant life in a limited area. The day before this field trip he went out and pulled up every plant in the area which he did not know.** This delimited our learning possibilities to what the professor knew in advance.

If he had not assumed the role of an authority, we could have all learned from each other, and the professor might even have learned from some of us. We do the same thing when we insist that students confine themselves to the textbook.

An essential is something which someone in authority has decided must be learned by everybody on authority. It is an absolute good, else it would not be essential. The fact seems to be that in our becoming world, some of the essentials are bound to be missed by some people, others by others. It would thus appear that there is no item of human knowledge that somebody could not get along without. We say that everyone must learn to read, but reading is not knowledge itself, but a tool for obtaining knowledge. It is a fine tool, and each of us will have his powers greatly enhanced by it.

While many of us have lived happy and successful lives without ever learning to read, it surely is a useful tool of which each of us should strive to get control. It will increase the possibility of our knowing, and to know is to add further to our powers. Even after we have learned to read, we are confronted with such a mass of miscellaneous reading material that we can never get much of it, and no two of us can get the same. There are certain big masses of information which we would probably be unable to miss, but not one of these would necessarily make or break us.

Subject Matter Alone Cannot Educate

Subject matter set out to be learned can be learned to a degree. It can be briefly stored against examination day, but unless it attains more meaning than the requirements of that day—unless its meaning takes on importance to the learning person—it will not abide long. In fact, it might be said not to have been learned at all, but perhaps only memorized, since when we learn, a modification of the organism is said to occur. That is, the organism behaves differently after true learning has taken place.

Certainly the acquiring of such subject matter cannot be said to be educational in itself. We all know people who have acquired much subject matter and have remained uneducated. We use the contradictory term "educated fools" in describing them. Something more than superficial acquisition seems to be necessary to make knowledge function, and to produce the educated man. This integration, being individual and personal, cannot be coerced, even by the person doing the learning. He cannot even coerce himself. This will be a great blow to many teachers, because they have proceeded on the theory that if they kept Johnny in after school and *made* him learn one of the teacher's absolutes, he would become educated.

The Fragmentation of Knowledge

Perception and its resulting reality is definitely related to wholes. We extract meaning from our surroundings as a whole. This meaning is as broad as life itself. It cannot be felt or understood in segments. So accustomed are we to comprehending wholes that we seem to have little power to put separate pieces together. If we want to get a better prognosis of a particular item in our surroundings, we may try to single it out, briefly and to a degree, but never entirely, except in schools or laboratories. As I walk to the office, I call upon science, language, mathematics, history, geography, and the rest all together. Especially is this true if I have to solve any special problem in the act. It would seem then that these special bits of knowledge ought not to be separated out by themselves in school but situations should be approached as wholes, with all the elements involved. Thus would mathematics, for example, become a living reality in use, rather than an abstraction for which the learner sees little use. It might be difficult thus to teach twelve-year-olds to invert the divisor and multiply in order to divide one fraction by another. But then maybe a twelve-year-old does not need to know how to divide one fraction by another. Even if he might need it sometime, there seems doubt that he can truly learn it, and so should not have his living clouded by it.

If we want to produce whole men, we will have to abandon our efforts to train or educate them in parts. We will have to stop doing things to him to train his memory, his will power, his reasoning power, etc. When a man meets a problem in his becoming world, he meets it with all he has—foot, ear, fist, purpose, value. These have to be marshalled together to meet not some, but all phases of the problem. Psychologists have long known this, but we teach just as though it had never been discovered. Some psychologists even teach that fact by a method which belies their belief in it.

Children Should Experience All Kinds of People

In school, we fragmentize our child society much as we do what we set out to be learned. Whereas in life whole men meet and cope with all kinds of people, children really meet only those who are their own age, often to the half year, and frequently are further placed only with children of the same ability in dealing with abstractions. Not uncommonly they are placed only with those of their own sex. The perceptions possible under such isolated circumstances are bound to give an incomplete picture of life as it must be lived. Selections are artificially made in advance.

This is perhaps logical if we believe, as we seem to, that education is a solitary, not a social process. What we have learned of perception and its personal nature should most certainly result in the rejection of this idea. If the school is to be unsocial, and we cannot educate each one in a solitary cubicle, then the next best we can do is to place the child with people who are as nearly like himself as possible. We aim at the most obvious similarities, age, sex, and ability according to our measuring scales.

But man is a social being, either by nature or by force of circumstance, and his problem of adjustment is with other people even more than with things. It is difficult for him to get communion with another being as discussed in Chapter IV, which he must have to a degree if he is to be truly social. No item of surroundings, thing or fact, can ever be the same to teacher as to learner, or to two different learners, no matter how much we group them on the basis of similarities. So it would appear that to educate a child he should be thrown with as many different kinds of people as possible. He should meet them as whole people, faced with concrete problems. The social needs of man and the difficulty of communion would demand that learners help one another, and that solutions should be reached by the best means available, not the hard way. The cooperative way of life, calling for mutual help and appreciation of different points of view, cannot be achieved in isolation.

School as Preparation

Since life is a becoming process, ever novel and ever personal, preparation for life (as our schools would do it) becomes impossible. We cannot store up a whole situation. It is true that the adult, in meeting a novel situation, uses his past experience. He will be prepared for it by the degree to which he can be given experiences which bear upon it. If a child in school can be given a rich variety of experiences, close to the concrete, he may have the experiential background needed to cope with any given situation. This differs from attempting to store fragments of knowledge against later need, because fragments of knowledge, given as absolutes, never come into experiential consciousness. If they are in fact successfully stored at all, they lack the practicality of the concrete experience.

Instead of teaching a child of six to read because he will sometime need to read, we might let the need for reading come out of what he is doing. Rather than teach him arithmetic, as a thing apart, he could be allowed to develop its need. In fact, instead of dealing primarily with abstractions—letters, numbers, and the like (as we do now)—he might learn his abstractions in relation to and after the concretions from which they arise. In this case, the number of abstractions with which he would deal would be greatly reduced in number and increased in meaning.

Children Have Their Own Purposes

In Chapter III we gave great emphasis to the importance of valueful purpose. The purpose of the individual, which may be influenced by the codescript of the gene, is essential to the process of extracting meaning out of surroundings through perception. When we receive a stimulus pattern, we depend to a degree upon our past experience as to which of an infinity of coincidences or externalities we choose to attend to. But past experience is not enough to account for the fine selection of these coincidences which we make. If we had only our experience to guide us, we would have to pay attention to all the coincidences which came within our experience. We do not do this; we select only that part of the scene which has something to do with our purposes. So the meaning extracted from the scene is not only unique to the viewing person on account of this individual experiential background, but also because of unique purpose. This makes a perception doubly personal and subjective.

Perhaps there is no common practice in school that is so damaging, then, as our violation of the learner's purpose. Since we believe now that his purpose is really part of the machinery involved in perception, it becomes well-nigh impossible for him even to have experiences on the strength of purposes other than his own. So when we make children "learn" that for which they see no need, it is doubtful that learning goes on at all. Certain it is that he learns vastly more about teachers as people than he does about the abused subject matter. I use the word "abused" here because what the teacher sought to have learned probably has value, but here it becomes a sort of battleground or bone of contention, a pawn between two conflicting sets of purposes. Any bit of human knowledge, even the ablative absolute, deserves better treatment.

Responsibility, Citizenship, Discipline

If we teach in accordance with the student's purpose (and what we know about perception would seem to demand it) then we can only teach what the student can purpose to learn. Thus we have to abandon the "essentials." If we teach in accordance with the student's purpose to learn, then the problem of getting the young to assume responsibility arises. Whenever he does anything in response to his purpose, he has assumed responsibility, for it was *his* purpose, not the teacher's. When he does something in response to the purpose of another, he has not assumed responsibility, but he has obeyed orders. If the teacher is going to furnish the purpose, he must also assume the responsibility.

The good citizen must want to be a good citizen, or he will not be one. In order to do this he has to be able to see the good of his group, which he can only see to the extent that he has a chance to cooperate with his group and get experience in sharing the purposes of his group. Good citizens are well-disciplined, but if the discipline is going to be worthwhile it has to relate to his larger good as he adjusts, giving some but not all to the good of his associates. The discipline thus achieved is intrinsic to the life he is leading, rather than being imposed from above. It will not desert him when he is on his own.

We all know what happens when the young get away from long-imposed discipline. It is dangerous to be near the doorway when such a class is dismissed. If the children had been using their own purposes for what they were doing, they would not have been under imposed restriction, and would not have built up a "head of steam." Our society needs people who have had experience in *self*-control while they are young, so that they will have practice in exercising it when they are free from the teacher or parent.

Rewards and Punishment as Coercion

To get children to pursue our purposes we have invented a most elaborate system of rewards and punishments. These are all extrinsic, that is, they lie outside the task itself. We give Junior a nickel if he will eat his cereal, although there is no connection between nickel and cereal. Later we give him "A" if he works hard and successfully on his geometry, but the reward lies outside the geometry. When one works in response to his own purposes, the reward for success or the punishment for failure lies in the act itself, and in the good he had hoped to achieve. If a book is read, it should be read because finding out what is in the book brings satisfaction to the reader or has significance in use, not so he can report on a number of pages to the teacher.

In connection with purpose, the question of coercion arises. Coercion implies the inflicting of the will of one upon another. It can never bring about the best kind of learning. It is certain to be accompanied by many adverse associated learnings. The child may learn that the teacher is an undesirable person, for example. He may find that there are many ways to beat the game. It may be necessary to use coercion on rare occasions, more or less of an emergency nature, but we should know what we are doing when we use it, recognize that its uses are limited and that it is accompanied by many undesirable side learnings. The learner will still make his own selections from the current situation, and they are likely to be different from the ones desired by the coercing adult.

The Value of Mistakes

In true problem solving, the problem must be real, that is, it must be so contrived that its solution becomes important to the learner. It is the task of the teacher to contrive learning experiences, but not to coerce outcomes. The teacher who pretends not to control outcomes but does so, is more harmful than the overt autocrat, because children can learn more easily how to combat the autocrat. When a teacher contrives an experience, he must be willing to accept the fact that each student will get something different out of it, and that some will not profit by it at all.

The learning experience must provide for trial and error, with a recognition of the fact that more is often learned by what we do wrong than by what we do right. We miseducate almost universally in that we fail to realize the educative value of mistakes. We follow our children around to see to it that they do not do anything wrong. This does not take account of the fact that doing things wrong, with its attendant frustration, is the very essence of growth. Without error there is no call for contriving. If the problem is unreal, as in the ordinary arithmetic class, its answer becomes entirely unimportant. In any problem, real or unreal, it is the contriving, the cut-and-try, the failure followed by success, which adds to the experiential background of the learner.

What About Evaluation?

Evaluation constitutes a large part of our day at school. There is of course nothing wrong with evaluation in itself. It is part of the very flow of life. Every time we make a choice we make an evaluation. Even when we select what we will attend to in the perception we entertain, we are evaluating. But note that it is *our* evaluation, not one made by someone else. The purposing, contriving learner should make his own evaluations, reflected in the satisfaction of the purposes which he feels. What I do may be evaluated by my colleagues as it affects them, and my social or unsocial conduct may be reflected in their attitudes toward me. But this is different (more intrinsic) than evaluation as it is used in schools, where it is the basis for extrinsic reward or punishment and is part of the whole scheme of coercion, or getting learners to operate on purposes other than their own.

This is not to imply that the teacher should not make any evaluation of students at all, although his evaluation of his own procedures should be fully as fruitful. It means that much less of the teacher's and student's time should be thus spent. More time could then be spent on learning something to evaluate. The teacher's evaluations of students should test growth rather than the student's ability to give back abstractions; and they should be designed to help the student in his own realistic evaluation and to show how teacher and student together can bring their resources to bear on growth. The teacher should make use of new devices for ascertaining the student's degree of surety and his ability to contrive new responses in the face of failure and frustration. There would be no place for the altogether too common punitive motive in evaluation.

Learning must start with concretions—with what we may call the "how-to-do." It is in this world of action, since perceptions are directives for action, that new experiences are accumulated. Certain abstractions will be useful tools, and will naturally arise. Operating in this moving world of "how-to-do," the learner will be confronted with natural problems which he must solve. As he contrives he will do many things that will not work. This will call for re-evaluating what has been done, and new trials. The attempt, the evaluation, the success, all play their part in taking a person from inadequacy to adequacy. The whole process is growth in its widest meaning; growth which enables the whole organism to become more competent to cope with life.

* "What is Life?" Erwin Schroedinger, Macmillan, 1945.
** Admitted later in a careless moment of camaraderie.

INTUITIVE THINKING

by Jerome Bruner

From *The Process of Education* by Jerome Bruner (New York: Vintage Books, 1963). Copyright © 1960, 1977 by the President and Fellows of Harvard College. Reprinted by permission of Harvard University Press.

In most classrooms, at all grade levels, there is an emphasis on step-by-step, logical procedures, whether students are acquiring new skills, gathering information, or solving problems. Thinking analytically is valued and rewarded. Indeed, many consider a cogent analysis to be the highest achievement for a learner. But as Bruner argues in this selection from his classic treatise, learners also benefit from developing their intuition.

Intuitive Thinking

by Jerome Bruner

One can say many more concrete things about analytic thinking than about intuitive thinking. Analytic thinking characteristically proceeds a step at a time. Steps are explicit and usually can be adequately reported by the thinker to another individual. Such thinking proceeds with relatively full awareness of the information and operations involved. It may involve careful and deductive reasoning, often using mathematics or logic and an explicit plan of attack. Or it may involve a step-by-step process of induction and experiment, utilizing principles of research design and statistical analysis.

In contrast to analytic thinking, intuitive thinking characteristically does not advance in careful, well-defined steps. Indeed, it tends to involve maneuvers based seemingly on an implicit perception of the total problem. The thinker arrives at an answer, which may be right or wrong, with little if any awareness of the process by which he reached it. He rarely can provide an adequate account of how he obtained his answer, and he may be unaware of just what aspects of the problem situation he was responding to. Usually intuitive thinking rests on familiarity with the domain of knowledge involved and with its structure, which makes it possible for the thinker to leap about, skipping steps and employing short cuts in a manner that requires a later rechecking of conclusions by more analytic means, whether deductive or inductive.

The complementary nature of intuitive and analytic thinking should, we think, be recognized. Through intuitive thinking the individual may often arrive at solutions to problems which he would not achieve at all, or at best more slowly, through analytic thinking. Once achieved by intuitive methods, they should if possible be checked by analytic methods, while at the same time being respected as worthy hypotheses for such checking. Indeed, the intuitive thinker may even invent or discover problems that the analyst would not. But it may be the analyst who gives these problems the proper formalism. Unfortunately, the formalism of school learning has somehow devalued intuition. It is the very strong conviction of men who have been designing curricula, in mathematics and the sciences particularly, over the last several years that much more work is needed to discover how we may develop the intuitive gifts of our students from the earliest grades onwards. For, as we have seen, it may be of the first importance to establish an intuitive understanding of materials before we expose our students to more traditional and formal methods of deduction and proof.

As to the nature of intuitive thinking, what is it? It is quite clear that it is not easy either to recognize a particular problem-solving episode as intuitive or, indeed, to identify intuitive ability as such. Precise definition in terms of observable behavior is not readily within our reach at the present time. Obviously, research on the topic cannot be delayed until such a time as a pure and unambiguous definition of intuitive thinking is possible, along with precise techniques for identifying intuition when it occurs. Such refinement is the goal of research, not its starting place. It suffices as a start to ask whether we are able to identify certain problem-solving episodes as more intuitive than others. Or, alternatively, we may ask if we can learn to agree in classifying a person's style or preferred mode of working as characteristically more analytic or inductive, on the one hand, or more intuitive, and, indeed, if we can find some way to classify tasks as ones that require each of those styles of attack. It is certainly clear that it is important not to confuse intuitive and other kinds of thinking with such evaluative notions as effectiveness and ineffectiveness: the analytic, the inductive, and the intuitive can be either. Nor should we distinguish them in terms of whether they produce novel or familiar outcomes, for again this is not the important distinction.

For a working definition of intuition, we do well to begin with Webster: "immediate apprehension or cognition." "Immediate" in this context is contrasted with "mediated"—apprehension or cognition that depends on the intervention of formal methods of analysis and proof. Intuition implies the act of grasping the meaning, significance, or structure of a problem or situation without explicit reliance on the analytic apparatus of one's craft. The rightness or wrongness of an intuition is finally decided not by intuition itself but by the usual methods of proof. It is the intuitive mode, however, that yields hypotheses quickly, that hits on combinations of ideas before their worth is known. In the end, intuition by itself yields a tentative ordering of a body of knowledge that, while it may generate a feeling that the ordering of facts is self-evident, aids principally by giving us a basis for moving ahead in our testing of reality.

Obviously, some intuitive leaps are "good" and some are "bad" in terms of how they turn out. Some men are good intuiters, others should be warned off. What the underlying heuristic of the good intuiter is, is not known but is eminently worthy of study. And what is involved in transforming explicit techniques into implicit ones that can be used almost automatically is a subject that is also full of conjecture. Unquestionably, experience and familiarity with a subject help—but the help is only for some. Those of us who teach graduate students making their first assault on a frontier of knowledge are often struck by our immediate reactions to their ideas, sensing that they are good or impossible or trivial before ever we know why we think so. Often we turn out to be right; sometimes we are victims of too much familiarity with past efforts. In either case, the intuition may be weeks or months ahead of the demonstration of our wisdom or foolhardiness. At the University of Buffalo there is a collection of successive drafts of poems written by leading contemporary poets. One is struck in examining them by the immediate sense one gets of the rightness of a revision a poet has made— but it is often difficult or impossible to say why the revision is better than the original, difficult for the reader and the poet alike.

It is certainly clear that procedures or instruments are needed to characterize and measure intuitive thinking, and that the development of such instruments should be pursued vigorously. We cannot foresee at this stage what the research tools will be in this field. Can one rely, for example, upon the subject's willingness to talk as he works, to reveal the nature of the alternatives he is considering, whether he is proceeding by intuitive leaps or by a step-by-step analysis or by empirical induction? Or will smaller-scale experimental approaches be suitable? Can group measurement procedures involving pencil and paper tests be used to provide a measure? All of these deserve a try.

What variables seem to affect intuitive thinking? There must surely be predisposing factors that are correlated with individual differences in the use of intuition, factors, even, that will predispose a person to think intuitively in one area and not in another. With respect to such factors, we can only raise a series of conjectures. Is the development of intuitive thinking in students more likely if their teachers think intuitively? Perhaps simple imitation is involved, or perhaps more complex processes of identification. It seems unlikely that a student would develop or have confidence in his intuitive methods of thinking if he never saw them used effectively by his elders. The teacher who is willing to guess at answers to questions asked by the class and then subject his guesses to critical analysis may be more apt to build those habits in his students than would a teacher who analyzes everything for the class in advance. Does the providing of varied experience in a particular field increase effectiveness in intuitive thinking in that field? Individuals who have extensive familiarity with a subject appear more often to leap intuitively into a decision or to a solution of a problem—one which later proves to be appropriate. The specialist in internal medicine, for example, may, upon seeing a patient for the first time, ask a few questions, examine the patient briefly, and then make an accurate diagnosis. The risk, of course, is that his method may lead to some big errors as well—bigger than those that result from the more painstaking, step-by-step analysis used by the young intern diagnosing the same case. Perhaps under these circumstances intuition consists in using a limited set of cues, because the thinker knows what things are structurally related to what other things. This is not to say that "clinical" prediction is better or worse than actuarial prediction, only that it is different and that both are useful.

In this connection we may ask whether, in teaching, emphasis upon the structure or connectedness of knowledge increases facility in intuitive thinking. Those concerned with the improvement of the teaching of mathematics often emphasize the importance of developing in the student an understanding of the structure or order of mathematics. The same is true for physics. Implicit in this emphasis, it appears, is the belief that such understanding of structure enables the student, among other things, to increase his effectiveness in dealing intuitively with problems.

What is the effect on intuitive thinking of teaching various so-called heuristic procedures? A heuristic procedure, as we have noted, is in essence a nonrigorous method of achieving solutions of problems. While heuristic procedure often leads to solution, it offers no guarantee of doing so. An algorithm, on the other hand, is a procedure for solving a problem which, if followed accurately, guarantees that in a finite number of steps you will find a solution to the problem if the problem has a solution. Heuristic procedures are often available when no algorithmic procedures are known; this is one of their advantages. Moreover, even when an algorithm is available, heuristic procedures are often much faster. Will the teaching of certain heuristic procedures facilitate intuitive thinking? For example, should students be taught explicitly, "When you cannot see how to proceed with the problem, try to think of a simpler problem that is similar to it; then use the method for solving the simpler problem as a plan for solving the more complicated problem"? Or should the student be led to learn such a technique without actually verbalizing it to himself in that way? It is possible, of course, that the ancient proverb about the caterpillar who could not walk when he tried to say how he did it may apply here. The student who becomes obsessively aware of the heuristic rules he uses to make his intuitive leaps may reduce the process to an analytic one. On the other hand, it is difficult to believe that general heuristic rules—the use of analogy, the appeal to symmetry, the examination of limiting conditions, the visualization of the solution—when they have been used frequently will be anything but a support to intuitive thinking.

Should students be encouraged to guess, in the interest of learning eventually how to make intelligent conjectures? Possibly there are certain kinds of situations where guessing is desirable and where it may facilitate the development of intuitive thinking to some reasonable degree. There may, indeed, be a kind of guessing that requires careful cultivation. Yet, in many classes in school, guessing is heavily penalized and is associated somehow with laziness. Certainly one would not like to educate students to do nothing but guess, for guessing should always be followed up by as much verification and confirmation as necessary; but too stringent a penalty on guessing may restrain thinking of any sort and keep it plodding rather than permitting it to make occasional leaps. May it not be better for students to guess than to be struck dumb when they cannot immediately give the right answer? It is plain that a student should be given some training in recognizing the plausibility of guesses. Very often we are forced, in science and in life generally, to act on the basis of incomplete knowledge; we are forced to guess. According to statistical decision theory, actions based on inadequate data must take account of both probability and costs. What we should teach students to recognize, probably, is when the cost of not guessing is too high, as well as when guessing itself is too costly. We tend to do the latter much better than the former. Should we give our students practice not only in making educated guesses but also in recognizing the characteristics of plausible guesses provided by others—knowing that an answer at least is of the right order of magnitude, or that it is possible rather than impossible? It is our feeling that perhaps a student would be given considerable advantage in his thinking, generally, if he learned that there were alternatives that could be chosen that lay somewhere between truth and complete silence. But let us not confuse ourselves by failing to recognize that there are two kinds of self-confidence—one a trait of personality, and another that comes from knowledge of a subject. It is no particular credit to the educator to help build the first without building the second. The objective of education is not the production of self-confident fools.

Yet it seems likely that effective intuitive thinking is fostered by the development of self-confidence and courage in the student. A person who thinks intuitively may often achieve correct solutions, but he may also be proved wrong when he checks or when others check on him. Such thinking, therefore, requires a willingness to make honest mistakes in the effort to solve problems. One who is insecure, who lacks confidence in himself, may be unwilling to run such risks.

Observations suggest that in business, as the novelty or importance of situations requiring decision increases, the tendency to think analytically also increases. Perhaps when the student sees the consequences of error as too grave and the consequences of success as too chancy, he will freeze into analytic procedures even though they may not be appropriate. On these grounds, one may wonder whether the present system of rewards and punishments as seen by pupils in school actually tends to inhibit the use of intuitive thinking. The assignment of grades in school typically emphasizes the acquisition of factual knowledge, primarily because that is what is most easily evaluated; moreover, it tends to emphasize the correct answer, since it is the correct answer on the straightforward examination that can be graded as "correct." It appears to us important that some research be undertaken to learn what would happen to the development of intuitive thinking if different bases for grading were employed.

Finally, what can be said about the conditions in which intuitive thinking is likely to be particularly effective? In which subjects will mastery be most aided by intuitive procedures followed by checking? Many kinds of problems will be best approached by some combination of intuitive and other procedures, so it is also important to know whether or not both can be developed within the same course by the same teaching methods. This suggests that we examine the mode of effective operation of intuition in different kinds of fields. One hears the most explicit talk about intuition in those fields where the formal apparatus of deduction and induction is most highly developed—in mathematics and physics. The use of the word "intuition" by mathematicians and physicists may reflect their sense of confidence in the power and rigor of their disciplines. Others, however, may use intuition as much or more. Surely the historian, to take but one example, leans heavily upon intuitive procedures in pursuing his subject, for he must select what is relevant. He does not attempt to learn or record everything about a period; he limits himself to finding or learning predictively fruitful facts which, when combined, permit him to make intelligent guesses about what else went on. A comparison of intuitive thinking in different fields of knowledge would, we feel, be highly useful.

We have already noted in passing the intuitive confidence required of the poet and the literary critic in practicing their crafts; the need to proceed in the absence of specific and agreed-upon criteria for the choice of an image or the formulation of a critique. It is difficult for a teacher, a textbook, a demonstration film, to make explicit provision for the cultivation of courage in taste. As likely as not, courageous taste rests upon confidence in one's intuitions about what is moving, what is beautiful, what is tawdry. In a culture such as ours, where there is so much pressure toward uniformity of taste in our mass media of communication, so much fear of idiosyncratic style, indeed a certain suspicion of the idea of style altogether, it becomes the more important to nurture confident intuition in the realm of literature and the arts. Yet one finds a virtual vacuum of research on this topic in educational literature.

The warm praise that scientists lavish on those of their colleagues who earn the label "intuitive" is major evidence that intuition is a valuable commodity in science and one we should endeavor to foster in our students. The case for intuition in the arts and social studies is just as strong. But the pedagogic problems in fostering such a gift are severe and should not be overlooked in our eagerness to take the problem into the laboratory. For one thing, the intuitive method, as we have noted, often produces the wrong answer. It requires a sensitive teacher to distinguish an intuitive mistake—an interestingly wrong leap—from a stupid or ignorant mistake, and it requires a teacher who can give approval and correction simultaneously to the intuitive student. To know a subject so thoroughly that he can go easily beyond the textbook is a great deal to ask of a high school teacher. Indeed, it must happen occasionally that a student is not only more intelligent than his teacher but better informed, and develops intuitive ways of approaching problems that he cannot explain and that the teacher is simply unable to follow or re-create for himself. It is impossible for the teacher properly to reward or correct such students, and it may very well be that it is precisely our more gifted students who suffer such unrewarded effort. So along with any program for developing methods of cultivating and measuring the occurrence of intuitive thinking, there must go some practical consideration of the classroom problems and the limitations on our capacity for encouraging such skills in our students. This, too, is research that should be given all possible support.

These practical difficulties should not discourage psychologists and teachers from making an attack on the problem. Once we have obtained answers to various of the questions raised in this chapter, we shall be in a much better position to recommend procedures for overcoming some of the difficulties.

THE UNLIVED LIFE

by Sylvia Ashton-Warner

From *Teacher* by Sylvia Ashton-Warner (New York: Simon & Schuster, 1963). Copyright © 1963 by Sylvia Ashton-Warner. Reprinted with the permission of Simon & Schuster.

Sylvia Ashton-Warner developed her own approach to instruction when she was teaching very young Maori children in an infant room (primary-grade classroom) in rural New Zealand. Finding that her pupils could not easily relate to standard-issue textbooks, she had them learn to read their own favorite words, write about what was most important to them, and share their writings with one another. She called this "organic" instruction because what she taught grew naturally from the children's lives outside of school—in the "pa," or the native community. Such an approach became more widespread in New Zealand and elsewhere many years later, but Ashton-Warner's deviation from the professional norm of her day was controversial. At that time, teachers were expected to use government-approved readers to develop literacy. Such books, still popular in schools today, feature Dick and Jane, Jack and Janet, or other such characters in various fictional adventures. With their spare style ("Look! Look! See Spot run!"), the materials are supposed to make learning to read easy, but Ashton-Warner believed the result was deadening. In this excerpt from her book, she reflects on why she devised her organic approach in response.

The Unlived Life

by Sylvia Ashton-Warner

It's all so merciful on a teacher, this appearance of the subjects of an infant room in the creative vent. For one thing, the drive is no longer the teacher's but the children's own. And for another, the teacher is at last with the stream and not against it: the stream of children's inexorable creativeness. As Dr. Jung says, psychic life is a world power that exceeds by many times all the powers of the earth; as Dr. Burrow says, the secret of our collective ills is to be traced to the suppression of creative ability; and as Erich Fromm says, destructiveness is the outcome of the unlived life.

So it is of more than professional moment that all of the work of young children should be through the creative vent. It is more than a teaching matter or a dominion one. It's an international matter. So often I have said, in the past, when a war is over the statesmen should not go into conference with one another but should turn their attention to the infant rooms, since it is from there that comes peace or war. And that's how I see organic teaching. It helps to set the creative pattern in a mind while it is yet malleable, and in this role is a humble contribution to peace.

The expansion of a child's mind can be a beautiful growth. And in beauty are included the qualities of equilibrium, harmony and rest. There's no more comely word in the language than "rest." All the movement in life, and out of it too, is towards a condition of rest. Even the simple movement of a child "coming up."

I can't disassociate the activity in an infant room from peace and war. So often I have seen the destructive vent, beneath an onslaught of creativity, dry up under my eyes. Especially with the warlike Maori five-year-olds who pass through my hands in hundreds, arriving with no other thought in their heads other than to take, break, fight and be first. With no opportunity for creativity they may well develop, as they did in the past, with fighting as their ideal of life. Yet all this can be expelled through the creative vent, and the more violent the boy the more I see that he creates, and when he kicks the others with his big boots, treads on fingers on the mat, hits another over the head with a piece of wood or throws a stone, I put clay in his hands, or chalk. He can create bombs if he likes or draw my house in flame, but it is the creative vent that is widening all the time and the destructive one atrophying, however much it may look to the contrary. And anyway I have always been more afraid of the weapon unspoken than of the one on a blackboard.

With all this in mind therefore I try to bring as many facets of teaching into the creative vent as possible, with emphasis on reading and writing. And that's just what organic teaching is; all subjects in the creative vent.

It's just as easy for a teacher, who gives a child a brush and lets him paint, to give him a pencil and let him write, and to let him pass his story to the next one to read. Simplicity is so safe. There's no occasion whatever for the early imposition of a dead reading, a dead vocabulary. I'm so afraid of it. It's like a frame over a young tree making it grow in an unnatural shape. It makes me think of that curtailment of a child's expansion of which Erich Fromm speaks, of that unlived life of which destructiveness is the outcome. "And instead of the wholeness of the expansive tree we have only the twisted and stunted bush." The trouble is that a child from a modern respectable home suffers such a serious frame on his behaviour long before he comes near a teacher. Nevertheless I think that after a year of organic work the static vocabularies can be used without misfortune. They can even, under the heads of external stimulus and respect for the standard of English, become desirable.

But only when built upon the organic foundation. And there's hardly anything new in the conception of progress from the known to the unknown. It's just that when the inorganic reading is imposed first it interferes with integration; and it's upon the integrated personality that everything is built. We've lost the gracious movement from the inside outward. We overlook the footing. I talk sometimes about a bridge from the pa to the European environment, but there is a common bridge for a child of any race and of more moment than any other: the bridge from the inner world outward. And that is what organic teaching is. An indispensable step in integration. Without it we get this one-patterned mind of the New Zealand child, accruing from so much American influence of the mass-mind type. I think that we already have so much pressure towards sameness through radio, film and comic outside the school, that we can't afford to do a thing inside that is not toward individual development, and from this stance I can't see that we can indulge in the one imposed reading for all until the particular variety of a mind is set. And a cross-section of children from different places in New Zealand provides me with an automatic check on the progress of the one-patterned mind. (I own seventy fancy-dress costumes which I lend.) All the children want the same costumes. If you made dozens of cowboy and cow-girl costumes, hundreds of Superman and thousands of Rocket Man costumes and hired them at half a guinea a go, you'd get every penny of it and would make a fortune vast enough to retire on and spend the rest of your life in the garden. As for my classics—Bo-Peep, the Chinese Mandarin, Peter Pan and the Witch and so on—they so gather the dust that they have had to be folded and put away. It's this sameness in children that can be so boring. So is death boring.

To write peaceful reading books and put them in an infant room is not the way to peace. They don't even scratch the surface. No child ever asked for a Janet or a John costume. There is only one answer to destructive-ness and that is creativity. And it never was and never will be any different. And when I say so I am in august company.

The noticeable thing in New Zealand society is the body of people with their inner resources atrophied. Seldom have they had to reach inward to grasp the thing that they wanted. Everything, from material requirements to ideas, is available ready-made. From mechanical gadgets in the shops to sensation in the films they can buy almost anything they fancy. They can buy life itself from the film and radio—canned life.

And even if they tried to reach inward for something that maybe they couldn't find manufactured, they would no longer find anything there. They've dried up. From babyhood they have had shiny toys put in their hands, and in the kindergartens and infant rooms bright pictures and gay material. Why conceive anything of their own? There has not been the need. The capacity to do so has been atrophied and now there is nothing there. The vast expanses of the mind that could have been alive with creative activity are now no more than empty vaults that must, for comfort's sake, be filled with non-stop radio, and their conversation consists of a list of platitudes and clichés.

I can't quite understand why.

From what I see of modern education the intention is just the opposite: to let children grow up in their own personal way into creative and interesting people. Is it the standard textbooks? Is it the consolidation? Is it the quality of the teachers? Is it the access to film and radio and the quality of those luxuries? Or is it the access to low-grade reading material infused through all of these things? I don't know where the intention fails but we end up with the same pattern of a person in nine hundred ninety-nine instances out of a thousand.

I said to a friend of mine, a professor, recently, "What kind of children arrive at the University to you?" He said,

"They're all exactly the same." "But," I said, "how can it be like that? The whole plan of primary education at least is for diversity." "Well," he answered, "they come to me like samples from a mill. Not one can think for himself. I beg them not to serve back to me exactly what I have given to them. I challenge them sometimes with wrong statements to provoke at least some disagreement but even that won't work." "But," I said, "you must confess to about three per cent originality." "One in a thousand," he replied. "One in a thousand."

On the five-year-old level the mind is not yet patterned and it is an exciting thought. True, I often get the over-disciplined European five, crushed beyond recognition as an identity, by respectable parents, but never Maoris, as a rule a five-year-old child is not boring. In an infant room it is still possible to meet an interesting, unpatterned person. "In the infant room," I told this professor, "we still have identity. It's somewhere between my infant-room level and your university level that the story breaks. But I don't think it is the plan of education itself."

I think that the educational story from the infant room to the university is like the writing of a novel. You can't be sure of your beginning until you have checked it with your ending. What might come of infant teachers visiting the university and professors visiting the infant room? I had two other professors in my infant room last year and they proved themselves to be not only delightfully in tune but sensitively helpful.

Yet what I believe and what I practise are not wholly the same thing. For instance, although I have reason to think that a child's occupation until seven should not be other than creative in the many mediums, nevertheless I find myself teaching some things.

With all this in mind, therefore, the intent of the infant room is the nurturing of the organic idea,

the preservation of the inner resources,

the exercise of the inner eye and

the protraction of the true personality.

I like unpredictability and variation; I like drama and I like gaiety; I like peace in the world and I like interesting people, and all this means that I like life in its organic shape and that's just what you get in an infant room where the creative vent widens. For this is where style is born in both writing and art, for art is the way you do a thing and an education based on art at once flashes out style.

The word "jalopy" made its fascinating appearance the other day. Brian wrote, "I went to town. I came back on a jalopy bus." This word stirred us. The others cross-questioned him on the character of such a bus. It turned out to mean "rackety" and although the word was picked up at once nevertheless they still ask for it to go up on the spelling list. We haven't had "jalopy" for spelling lately, Brian says. He loves spelling it, which is what I mean when I say that the drive is the children's own. It's all so merciful on a teacher.

IMPROVING EDUCATION WITH GAMES

by Clark C. Abt

From *Serious Games* by Clark C. Abt (New York: The Viking Press, 1970). Copyright © 1970 by Abt Associates, Inc. Reprinted by permission of Clark C. Abt.

Clark Abt founded Abt Associates in 1965 to develop simulation games for a variety of purposes, including management training, business forecasting, systems analysis, and classroom learning. Although the use of such games in schools and other organizations is not commonplace, most people who have participated in them are convinced of their value for developing topic knowledge, relevant experience, and a variety of thinking abilities. In this excerpt from his book on the subject, Abt reflects on the particular merit of these "serious games" for students.

Please note that Abt's remark about "Chapters I and IV" in this selection is a reference to chapters of his book, not chapters of this volume.

Improving Education with Games

by Clark C. Abt

In contemporary formal education, there appear to be many serious gaps between what is considered worth knowing and what is needed for an effective life. This discrepancy between instructional practice and postschool practicality is attested by the repeated worldly success of mediocre students and the quite modest worldly accomplishments of many outstanding students.

There are even more serious gaps between how knowledge and methods—worthwhile or not—are taught in the schools and how they are most effectively learned in life, indicated in part by the abandonment of free high-school education by over one-quarter of the teen-age population that voluntarily drops out before graduation. America's educational system suffers from motivational, scholarly, intuition-building, social-behavior-training, evaluation, research, planning, and program-development inadequacies.

The motivational inadequacies are probably in most urgent need of repair. To be motivated is to have a reason for action. The first-grade student, upon entering school for the first time, brings with him a set of values and "reasons for action" established by his parents. He may be positively motivated toward learning, negatively motivated, or simply unmotivated. Though the educational system can never hope to negate the influences of home environment, it can modify these influences in many respects. The highly motivated student can overcome the most unimaginative school curriculum, the most banal school texts, and the most limited facilities if he has the encouragement of his family and his teacher. But in many cases, the educational environment being so restrictive, the teacher feels helpless and becomes unmotivated himself, simply waiting for the end of the school year to find a better school or a better job. In these cases, when the student moves on to higher grades, he is often far less motivated than he once was. But it is obvious that the negatively motivated or unmotivated student suffers most. For if he is not provided with imaginative and exciting "reasons for action" within the school, he will soon find school a waste of time—it interferes with his "reasons for action" outside of school. It is not relevant to his daily life and has not been made relevant by the curriculum, texts, or, most importantly, the teacher.

This problem of motivation, particularly in the elementary grades, becomes more significant when one realizes that the attitudes and skills developed in young children determine their later performance. Most students who do poorly in high school could have been identified early in elementary school.

Students who are not motivated to learn in school are frequently highly motivated in their other activities. Even the youngest children play with a vengeance cops-and-robbers, hide-and-seek, cowboys-and-Indians, and other competitive games. The differences in these two environments, at least in the degree of attention and interest in participating, are partially explained by the great drama in the play environment and the frequent lack of drama in the school environment. This "drama" involves *conflicts* of *uncertain outcome* among actors with whom the child can identify; in playing games, children "become" the characters they represent, and engage vicariously in the conflicts their roles afford. The application of these exciting elements to activities in the school can stimulate the child to learn new intellectual concepts.

Most social, economic, and historical material is full of conflicts of interest. The student's identification with the characters or groups involved in such real-life problems is usually rapid and strong, since students so often deal with uncertainty and conflict in their own lives. And planning, playing, and analyzing educational games motivates the students to study the issues dramatized in the games and the literature dealing with these issues, to synthesize solutions to the problems posed, and to evaluate critically the solutions developed in the process.

I was once given a particularly impressive indication of this motivational effect of simulation games. It happened in the course of demonstrating a game called "Grand Strategy" to some junior-high-school students and teachers in Vancouver, Washington.[1] The game simulates some events of World War I.

Ten players represented the chiefs of state of ten major nations involved in World War I. Each player's objective was to achieve his nation's political aims at the least military and economic cost. Each player made ten moves simulating strategic decisions taken semiannually from 1914 through 1918. These moves consisted of players making and breaking alliances, deploying armies and navies, and initiating, responding to, and terminating hostilities. The players were seated facing a chalk-drawn map of Europe in 1914. Also posted were the open-alliance relations and the number and location of army divisions and naval fleets of all the powers.

In the morning's game, the war expanded through the entanglement of alliances, much as in the actual history of the prewar period. Just before lunch, the student players were told that they would get another chance to replay afterward. But instead of going to lunch, most of them went to the school library to study the history of World War I. It is possible that this added study paid off in problem-solving achievement. In the afternoon game, the students were able to keep the war from expanding and to reach a peaceful compromise solution to the international conflict. It might be said that in that one day they were motivated to learn more about how World War I started and ended, and how it might have been settled better, than they would have been taught by any other technique. John Dewey's ideal of the "active learner" was executed successfully.

The superior motivation of students in educational simulation games is widely recognized.[2] It is obvious that motivation is necessary but not sufficient for learning. But the educational benefits of simulation games other than motivational are only dimly understood. The training that games provide in intuition-building, problem-solving, and social behavior, for example, are of incalculable value.

Most complex processes in technology, economics, and politics include several subprocesses going on simultaneously, or "in parallel" in time. Assembly lines fed by subassembly lines operating simultaneously, simultaneous production and consumption in a market, and simultaneous competition for votes by two or more political candidates are all examples of these processes.

Describing such simultaneous interactions with printed or spoken words is difficult because it requires considerable abstraction and memorization—the learner has to remember that while A was going on, B was starting, and meanwhile C was doing something else, and D was tripped by B. It is like trying to describe a fast play in football with words to someone who, never having played or seen a football game, has limited powers of abstraction, memory, or retrieval of significant data at the right time.

The best way to learn about the parallel processes in a football game is to play it or, second-best, to simulate playing it by following it through in imagination. The same holds true for learning about other parallel processes in technology, economics, and politics. The inadequate instruction in parallel processes is often never remedied in many liberal-arts students in college, and the students' inability to comprehend and manipulate such abstractions creates an often impenetrable barrier to their making scientific analyses of complex systems problems. It probably also contributes to simplistic thinking in terms of one or two "causes" rather than a "systems" understanding of complex effects.

Another intellectual skill inadequately taught by conventional methods is allocation of resources. The basic idea is that, as with energy and matter in most instances, at any one time within any one system a constant amount of resources are conserved—more in one place means less in another. The "conservative system" of classical physics is also the fixed-resource budget of the economist—more expenditures on one thing mean less on another. The core issue is that of allocating limited resources to maximize one's objectives.

The economic concepts of satisfying minimum objectives[3] and optimizing achievement of residual objectives by allocations proportional to returns are rarely taught below the college level. But these concepts are implicit in most games in which limited resources must be allocated among competing objectives (such as in successive bids in poker), and explicit in such economic games as "Manchester" and "Empire" (described in Chapters I and IV), games that have been successfully played by schoolchildren.

The mathematical theory of games itself is to some extent a rigorous treatment of this type of problem.[4] And the logical analysis of decision-making under conditions of incomplete information or uncertainty is a further development of the mathematical game theory exemplified in most games of chance. This is an intellectual realm that is intensely relevant to most of life's decisions, but it is almost never taught below the college level and often is not even included in college liberal-arts curricula. The elementary study of probability and statistics offered in some high schools is not usually sufficient to relate the logical analysis of uncertainty to the decision-making process.

Perhaps the most seminal and pervasive concepts in mathematical game theory are those of "zero-sum" and "non-zero-sum" games, and the "social" or Pareto optimum. A zero-sum game is one in which the sum of the winners' and losers' payoffs (or gains) is always zero. This means that if one player in a two-person game (the mathematics of games explodes in complexity with increasing numbers of players) wins a certain amount, the other player must lose that same amount. If there are three players, and two win, the third player must lose the sum of the winnings of the other two. A non-zero-sum game is one in which the winner's gain is not necessarily at the cost of the loser. Both (or all) players can win, as in peace-keeping, or both can lose, as in nuclear war. Non-zero-sum games are more complex than zero-sum but more like life in that while encompassing the pure competitive aspects they also include the preservation of that game itself which is the "social" and mutual objective of the players. The best strategy in such games is one that maximizes the total wins of all players. This is sometimes called the "Pareto optimum," after the great mathematical economist Wilfredo Pareto, who first expressed this concept.

Conflict strategies are also a common aspect of human civilization that rarely receive attention in the classroom. Mathematical game theory, oligopoly theory of the business firm, and political-military strategic analysis all deal with conflict or competition for incompatible (zero-sum) objectives by adversaries. But competitive processes are also a part of everyday life, and an everyday part of uncommon but crucial moments, such as negotiations among lovers, labor and management, and governments.

It is no accident that the theory that provides a scientific, logical, and quantitative analysis of competitive processes is called "game" theory. Games are the formal equivalent of these competitive processes, stripped of most incidental details. Reducing large-scale competitive processes to simulation games exposes their essential dynamics with a lucidity and drama unequaled by other teaching techniques.[5]

Intuitive problem-solving is an aspect of education neglected almost everywhere except in multiple-choice tests. It is as if educators considered intuitive problem-solving the moral equivalent of uncontrolled bohemianism. Beats, hippies, and the alienated of all sorts extol intuition with an exaggeration matched only by the disdain many formal educators have for it. It needs to be understood that intuition, while no substitute for knowledge and education, is a valuable application of knowledge: generally, the quality of an intuitive insight is directly related to the amount of knowledge brought to the problem.

A naïve but useful definition of intuitive problem-solving might be that it is the kind of mental activity which is not self-conscious and is therefore difficult to reproduce or explain on demand, but which nevertheless occasionally integrates diverse facts and ideas in a fruitful way not previously apparent to rational, systematic analysis. As such, intuition is a very efficient but somewhat unreliable aid to problem-sensing and problem-solving. To become an effective learning tool, it needs to be stimulated, given expression, tested, and evaluated. Effective intuitions should be rewarded, while incorrect intuitions should be so determined by rational analysis and then discarded. In short, intuition should be developed to complement and advance rational analysis. In their fear of a romantic worship of intuition to the exclusion of rational analysis, educators have often rejected intuition wholesale.

Simulation games stimulate, reward, and judge intuitions according to pragmatic standards rather than doctrinal ones. Enlightening intuitions are rewarded for their superior problem-solving speed over systematic analysis. False intuitions prove to be ineffective in game play. The ideal problem-solving strategy that emerges for most players combines intuition and analysis—analysis used to check intuition, and intuition used to extend analysis beyond familiar limits.

Closely related to the need for instruction in intuition-building is the need for instruction "custom-fitted" to individual student capabilities. Public education by its very nature must be geared to educating the greatest possible number of students. Most students are near the "average" and find their schools not too badly suited to their needs and abilities. But public schools do not usually meet the needs of students far below or above the average. Many students are discouraged by material that is too difficult for them; superior students are bored by material that is too simple. Providing equal opportunity for all students, regardless of their unequal abilities or limitations, is one of the great difficulties of public education.

The one-to-one relationship between a skilled tutor and a student is, of course, ideal, but it is also impractically expensive. The self-directed learning provided by programmed instruction permits the pupil to proceed at his own pace, but it is cognitively and socially limiting: only the predetermined answers are acceptable, and this tends to limit programmed instruction to rote learning of simple facts. The excitement and encouragement generated by another human being is missing, as is the intelligent response to a novel solution. True interaction, which produces the most memorable kind of "feedback" in problem-solving, does not occur.

How then can instruction be individualized in an economical but nonlimiting way? Peer learning, or the direct instruction of students by other students, is one way which appears promising. In the Homework Helper program in New York City, for example, student instructors advanced even more than the students they tutored.

Peer instruction can be made still more efficient and intensive by using educational simulation games and small group projects. Students can simultaneously learn different things on different levels in the same game and probably learn them better than they would from an older teacher. In one game played in a ghetto school, for example, the students ranged from a nearly illiterate eleven-year-old to an advanced high-school senior. Both learned through the game about social change in an industrializing society, although on different levels of sophistication.

Individual instruction is aided by the many decision alternatives that must be confronted by the players in any effective educational game. Even relatively simple simulation games are sufficiently rich in content to provide several different levels of learning simultaneously to students of different abilities. The slow learners will concentrate on the concrete, static elements of the game. The moderately fast learners will develop concepts of cause and effect and attempt to apply them. The most advanced learners will consider the strategic interactions of several parallel causal chains.

Training students in acceptable social behavior is one of the schools' most important tasks, yet it is rarely accomplished realistically in the conventional classroom. Schools and teachers usually have predetermined values expressed in "Dress Codes," "Rules for the Playground," or "Student Handbooks." The values inherent in these rules or codes are imposed from above, and the student must obey or be punished. There is rarely an opportunity for cooperative problem-solving requiring student leadership and negotiation. These skills can be developed, however, through small-group or team activities in simulation games which improve cooperative social skills in concert, rather than in conflict, with cognitive ones.

Grading "on the curve,"[6] which occurs in most schools, is intrinsically competitive in an unproductive way. It reduces the matter of marks to a zero-sum game: every high mark given to one student makes it tougher for other students to also obtain a high mark. Many students seem to realize this instinctively, and thus achievement is inhibited because it is frowned on as "making things tough for the others." A more socially cooperative way of grading (making classroom learning a non-zero-sum game) would be to distribute the students into small teams competing for objective (rather than relative) achievement scores. These student "learning teams" would encourage cooperative problem-solving behavior among team members, while enjoying the motivating powers of team competition. One of the obvious ways the teams could interact would be in games.

Another type of socialization usually omitted from the classroom is that combination of competitive initiative, objective calculation, and courteous restraint which we call "sportsmanship." This may be learned on the playing fields and on the streets, but not all students learn it this way, and none now learn it in association with intellectual effort. The making of classroom learning into a team sport offers the possibilities of applying the best motivational and socializing values of athletics to competitive intellectual activities. It may also lend a kind of formal legitimization of adolescent values to the learning process itself.[7]

The evaluation of students is presently done by the teachers' grading, standardized tests, or a combination of the two. But the teachers may be biased, and standardized tests are given only rarely, possibly when a student is not at his best. On the whole, though, the two methods complement each other—except where they are applied to students for whom they are not designed, such as those of a different cultural background from the teachers and testers. Since conventional English-language skills are needed to do well on these tests, we can expect a non-English-speaking foreigner to perform poorly. Likewise, we can expect the "disadvantaged" student speaking a "public" or "nonstandard" English to do badly too. Obviously some culturally less specific instrument is needed for evaluation, and games may offer one such tool.

In the summer of 1965 I met some high-school drop-outs who were enrolled in a remedial course at Thompson Academy in Boston. They scored in the 80's on I.Q. tests and performed poorly enough in the classrooms to be regarded as "backward." Yet when several of these teen-agers participated in a game simulating the interactions of city block residents, racketeers, and police, they came suddenly alive and performed not only well, but brilliantly. It was clear to all of us that this performance was an indi-cator of a kind of problem-solving intelligence that had escaped conventional measurement.

Games could be used by schools to identify specific types of nonverbal abilities cognitive problem-solving, social negotiating, organizing, and communication skills.

This use of games to identify the superficially "back-ward" student who has good unexpressed intelligence is potentially very significant in several ways. Research has shown that many teachers tend to work most closely with students they believe to be "bright" and neglect those they believe to be "dull."[8] Teachers' expectations often become self-fulfilling prophecies, as the apparently bright students are stimulated further, and the apparently dull are "writ-ten off" to mere custodial care. But if games identify oth-erwise hidden intelligence in a student, he gains another chance for a better rating in his teacher's self-fulfilling suc-cess prophecy.

Also, "games testing" has great potential as a means of measuring skills that are extremely important in adult life but essentially untested in formal academic exams. If I were a company president hiring a manager or a general problem-solver, I would much rather observe a candidate's performance in a challenging, multiplayer game than in a conventional test, because the problem-solving needed in the game is much closer to that needed on the job than are the written tests.

Educational planning—of curricula, classroom schedules, instructional methods, teacher recruitment, school facilities and equipment utilization, and allocation of students to schools, etc.—is still largely a cut-and-dried kind of thing. The bold experimentation required is usually too costly in terms of time lost, dollars spent, administrative chaos, and potential damage to students. Experimenting, measuring the results, developing the theory, and verifying or correcting initial hypotheses are limited today largely to analyses of one or a few variables, with *ceterus paribus* assumptions for the rest.[9] But simulations or games offer an inexpensive and relatively unthreatening means of experimentation. The exercise of "manual" models (human-operated, as opposed to computer-operated) has, in fact, already aided in developing a quantitative, mathematical model, or manipulable theory, predicting student achievement changes, dropout rates, expected average lifetime earnings, and equality of educational opportunity as a result of teacher, materials, and facilities changes.[10]

In another instance, some forty school superintendents at the Central Michigan Education Research Center played a game the object of which was to acquaint them with the electronic possibilities for improving the efficiency of their schools. Within a few hours they successfully negotiated a plan to link together several diverse school districts with teletypes, educational TV, and a time-shared computer. A conventional conference would have used up days of diffuse talking without ever getting around to these specific solutions.

Another game simulated one crisis-ridden day in an experimental Job Corps center for women. The roles of students, staff, local citizens, and government visitors were simulated by the trainee players. Crises were introduced on a programmed basis and were responded to by them. After the simulation was over, they rated each other's performance according to various criteria of administrative efficiency, communicativeness, creativity, crisis management, etc., etc. The game revealed weaknesses of indecisiveness and insensitivity on the part of some candidates who had been very impressive in interviews, as well as the skills of others who did not seem capable in the interviews.

In education, there are no substitutes for highly motivated and creative teachers, relevant and exciting school texts, imaginative and well-planned curricula providing individualized instruction, and effective and well-designed school facilities and plants. But the day has not yet arrived in which all these ideals flourish in all school systems, and until that day does arrive, games will play an important role in educational life. Games are not a panacea for all the ills of the educational system today, but they do provide fast and effective relief for some of these ills. The challenges posed to educators by the problems involved in planning games force them to deal with new problems and to see old problems from larger or different perspectives. Thus games serve a creative as well as an analytic function in educational planning and programming.

The central idea of teaching with games, both in and out of the classroom, is to use the time spent in the classroom or doing homework to create a laboratory environment—an environment in which experiments can be made, hypotheses formulated, and new and better experiments planned. Games help to create this laboratory feeling by providing objectives and procedures. They also encourage imaginative freedom to experiment with alternative solutions, while at the same time offering a realistic set of constraints on less practical responses to problems. The students can learn not only by observing the results of games, but also by playing and indeed by designing them.

The first phase of game learning, the design and preparation stage, may be divided into two kinds of activities: relatively passive preparation for active game play, and the actual design of the game to be played. The former is likely to be more common, but the latter is probably more rewarding. The former involves simply learning the background material to be simulated in the game and the game rules. This is little different from conventional study, except that it tends to be highly motivated by virtue of the promise that one can express competitively and dramatically what one has learned, rather than merely regurgitating it in an examination.

In the latter, more rewarding way of game preparation, the game designer is actually inventing a simulation model process of the process to be gamed. (This is also what social scientists, economists, engineers, and mathematicians do when they simulate a complex problem in more manipulable and simplified form for the purpose of staging experiments impractical in the real world.) In the course of doing so, the student must identify the significant variables involved, the relationships among them, and the dynamics of the interaction. To do this successfully is, in fact, to understand the process being simulated and to be able, in large degree, to predict its results accurately. Involving the students in this process expands their knowledge greatly: they learn not only factual content but also the processes, relationships, and interactions involved.

The most obvious way to teach with games is to play them in the classroom. This raises the practical issues of topic selection, timing, logistic arrangements, casting, materials, special requirements imposed on teachers, and interactions with other curriculum materials and activities. Most topics are suitable for educational gaming, some more so than others: topics that involve multiple forces or actors in some form of mutual competition with uncertain outcomes are most gameable. On the other hand, some topics which may not seem ideally suited to being gamed may be so remote from the students' interests that some form of classroom activity is required to stimulate interest, in which case games are a useful motivating technique.

Many required classroom topics and subjects are best learned by direct study—reading, observation, or field experimentation. There is hardly any subject, however, that does not have some interactive, competitive elements that are natural material for gaming—and other relatively static and formal elements that strain the mechanism of the game. To integrate these elements one must first of all divide the material to be learned into those parts with interactive and competitive elements and those of a formal or static nature. If, for example, the students are studying the Constitution of the United States, what the Constitution actually says is learned best from reading it. But the story of how the Constitution was written, why certain parts were written one way or another, what some of the alternative ways and interpretations were, can be well understood by means of a Constitutional Convention game, in which the competing political and economic forces can be dramatically simulated. The reading can be left for home study, with the essential interaction among individual and autonomous decision-making players being the only activity that requires the students to be together. After all, the classroom is the only place where students can directly interact, and this ought to be fully exploited by means of the teaching device that makes use of these interactions—namely, the game.

Games stimulate conventional study and can be used to summarize the results by dramatizing the interaction of disparate elements that were studied in isolation. If a given classroom study topic usually requires ten classroom hours, one could begin with a one-hour game and append to the tenth a one- or two-hour game—the first devoted to exploring the topic and the second to analyzing the results of study.

Most teachers who have used classroom games are enthusiastic about them, but some are ambivalent, and a few are violently opposed. The use of games for teaching, it has been argued, requires both too much and too little. At an educational conference in 1965, for example, a former head of the American Federation of Teachers suggested that educational games would both keep teachers too busy to do their jobs, and at the same time threaten their jobs by taking away their work!

A teacher using educational games becomes more of a research director and coach than a lecturer and disciplinarian. The game mode carries with it its own rules of behavior or discipline which must be observed by the participants if they are to enjoy the interaction of the game. The peers of whatever age involved in the game rarely break these rules because they know that it will end the game for them. Rarely do children in baseball or football games let the game fall apart because they cannot abide by the rules. Children do not want to play games they do not like, following somebody else's rules, but they are generally happy to play, and often insist on playing, games they like by the rules of the game. The teacher in a games classroom, then, need not be a disciplinarian. The time and energy saved may be directed to coaching the students to play the games more effectively, or observing their intellectual strengths and weaknesses when faced with specific types of situations.

These concepts are not new. Maria Montessori suggested over fifty years ago that the teacher spend more time observing students and less time directing them. More recently John Holt has reaffirmed this concept of teaching, which is not so much permissive as analytical—that is, teaching is seen as an activity of analyzing and responding to student performance rather than a constant attempt to control it. In this kind of education, the teacher has a responsibility to be much more analytical and lucid in the presentation of the game mode and in the analysis of the game consequences than is usually required by the lecture system. In a class where games are used, the teacher must learn to give brief but very intensive analyses and explanations, interspersed with longer periods of observations of student experiments and occasional coaching remarks. This is entirely different from the continuous pattern of doctrinaire topical material transferred from textbooks to the teacher's mind to the teacher's mouth to the students' pencils. And it should be more rewarding and entertaining. The teacher is now an attendant, an audience at a drama in which student actors display their problem-solving capabilities in intellectual contests. There is suspense over the uncertainty of the outcome, and emotional identification with contesting actors. But the teacher is also the critic, evaluating each player's interpretation of his role.

The teacher need not worry about being disengaged from the students in their play of serious educational games, for he is game director-referee-coach throughout, and afterward acts as chairman of a "de-briefing" or postmortem game analysis. This post-game analysis should be a structured, directed discussion of the limitations and insights offered by the game and of the performance of the players in both representing and solving their problems effectively. Here the players will consider the teacher as a vital part of the game's operation and resolved meaning, rather than as a person who interferes with classroom activities.

Great demands are made on the teacher in understanding the processes being simulated and taught by the games, and in understanding and presenting fairly their most meaningful aspects. He must recognize the students' limitations in simplifying or neglecting some aspects of the processes simulated. But evaluation of students by means of the tiresome process of grading quizzes (which are often a better measure of how well a student writes than of how much he really knows) can be replaced at least in part by evaluation taking place *during* a game—evaluation by peers in the course of the game and by the teacher in both his observations and postgame analysis. Thus, a teacher's role becomes more demanding and interesting intellectually, and less demanding in routine clerical activity.

The timing of a classroom game should be made to maximize the game's dramatic impact on the students, either in terms of a culminating drama that weaves together diverse strands of one large topic, or as a way of introducing or making interesting and meaningful an otherwise abstract or uninteresting topic. Equally important is the timing of actions within the game itself. Here too the teacher-director has a crucial controlling function, for he has the power and, indeed, the responsibility to maintain the pace of the game so that maximal learning occurs. When the pace lags, he can often speed things up by introducing crises of various kinds. When players are indecisive or confused by too many trivial calculations, it is often effective to introduce a critical problem which demands immediate action from all the players or which affects their fortunes if action is not taken. In a political game, for example, the candidate teams contesting an election might be projected into more intensive activities if the referee announced that all campaign platforms must be presented on a simulated television program within the next few minutes. In an economics game, a temporary lag in buying and selling might be overcome by the referee's introducing a threat that affects them differentially, such as the loss of a given stockpile of goods or the sudden entry of a major buyer.

Disputes not covered by rules frequently arise in simulation games which allow liberally for individual players' imaginations. Where the interpretations of roles or parts in the game are left to the individuals, conflicting interpretations may arise. The good game director or referee will resolve these disputes as quickly and equitably—also as quietly—as possible. Interruption of the other activities of the game should be avoided by isolating the disputants from the rest of the game, resolving the crisis, or agreeing to resolve it after the game and requesting the players to go on with what they were doing. The author found that, in general, the best ground rule for settling unanticipated disputes is to resolve them on grounds that most closely correspond to the reality being simulated.

The scoring of a game is, of course, extraordinarily important. Players should be able to determine the relative effectiveness of their playing, who won or lost (or played realistically or unrealistically), and what effective play means in the particular process being simulated in the game. Scoring also provides what psychologists call "closure" to the activity, completing it in a psychologically satisfactory way.

Scoring can be done by a referee, the players themselves, or a combination of the two. In our experience, player scoring has been the most effective for educational and analytical purposes, because the details of effective and ineffective performance are closely scrutinized in the process. It requires all the players to have a clear and common understanding of the "win criteria" of the game, the penalties for violations of the rules, and the overall game purposes. In many complex simulation games, scoring cannot be reduced to a simple matter of assigning point values on the basis of a predetermined schedule to various types of behavior. It usually requires interpretation of the relative effectiveness of different moves both in terms of the realism with which they simulated the process under study and the effectiveness of the response in terms of the win criteria.

The scoring activity is related to but not identical with the evaluation of the game itself or of the players. The scoring is rarely an indication of effectiveness. Thus, a player who makes many effective decisions in a game and scores high has demonstrated operationally his comprehension of the process being simulated, but the converse is not true. A player not effectively responding to the game situation in terms of the decisions he makes is not necessarily stupid or ignorant; he may have had something in mind that simply could not be expressed in the framework of the game. He may have believed that his ineffective responses were the most accurate possible representation of his role.

Similarly, games often identify intelligence, general problem-solving ability, dramatic talent, and negotiating talent in individuals who have difficulty demonstrating these capacities on ordinary intelligence and aptitude tests. But the absence of such talent in a simulation game is not necessarily significant; the player may have been unable to apply his particular skills in the context of the game.

In the course of game play, students will sometimes develop innovative and completely unanticipated solutions to problems. When this occurs, it is important that the teacher be flexible about game scoring. Usually a trade-off must be made—some students will consider the game unfair because it has not been scored completely by the predetermined criteria while others will feel that really creative thinking should be rewarded. Explaining the significance of the unexpected behavior and the reasons it deserves to be considered with the predetermined criteria is usually required.

Game performances, like dramatic performances, may be good, bad, or indifferent. The game content also, like the script of a play, may be evaluated as good, bad, or indifferent. If the game itself and the substance of it is given a low rating by the players, redesign and replay are obviously called for to better the simulation and approach the analytical objectives more closely. In this sense, the scoring of the entire game rather than of individual players is an essential part of the process that leads to a redesign and refinement of simulation games.

Footnotes:

(1) The demonstration was sponsored by the Northwest Regional Educational Laboratories, Portland, Oregon.

(2) See Sarane Boocock and E. O. Schild, *Simulation Games in Learning* (Beverly Hills, California: Sage Publications, 1968).

(3) In the jargon of the mathematical operations researcher, sometimes called "satisficing," perhaps to combine the suggestions of satisfying and sufficing.

(4) John Von Neuman and Oskar Morgenstern in *The Theory of Games and Economic Behavior* (Princeton, New Jersey: Princeton University Press, 1953) present the basic logic and mathematics of both serious (such as duels) and nonserious (such as poker) games. The book, a mathematical and philosophical classic, is not exactly light reading, although much of it is comprehensible to any interested reader.

(5) The outstanding work illustrating the applications and limitations of game theory is T. C. Schelling's *Strategy of Conflict* (Cambridge, Massachusetts: Harvard University Press, 1960). In this seminal book, Schelling applies mathematical economics game theory concepts to duels, competitions, and wars. Another lucid treatment—less value-free but useful as an introduction to the subject—is Anatol Rapoport's *Fights, Games, and Debates* (Ann Arbor: University of Michigan Press, 1960).

(6) "Grading on the curve" means giving a class of students grades on the basis of their relative position to each other on a statistical distribution of all the raw test scores in the class. The top ten per cent may get an A, the bottom ten per cent an F, and so on.

(7) James S. Coleman, in his book *The Adolescent Society* (New York: Free Press, 1961), discusses how the teen-age peer culture tends to inhibit academic achievement, and how athletic contests might be mobilized for academic purposes. Professor Coleman is a leading

designer of educational games for teaching the social sciences, as well as a distinguished sociologist.

(8) Also known as the Rosenthal effect, after its principal investigator, Professor Richard Rosenthal of Harvard University.

(9) One notable exception is the U.S. Office of Education report *Equality of Educational Opportunity* (U.S. Government Printing Office, 1966), also known as the Coleman Report after its principal author.

(10) Clark C. Abt, "Design for an Elementary and Secondary Education Cost-Effectiveness Model." (Abt Associates, Inc., Cambridge, Massachusetts, 1967).

THE WITHERING
OF CURIOSITY

by Thomas French

From *South of Heaven: Welcome to High School at
the End of the Twentieth Century* by Thomas French
(New York: Doubleday, 1993). Copyright © 1993
by Thomas French. Used by permission of
Doubleday, a division of Bantam Doubleday Dell
Publishing Group, Inc.

The climate of the classroom and of the school can have quite a lot to do with how well students learn. Some need a warm, comfortable environment; others thrive on invigorating challenges; still others do their best when they are enveloped in cool serenity. Although many teachers and students have an intuitive feel for the climate of a class or a school, they have less understanding of how it developed, how it affects students and teachers, and what can be done to maintain it, if it is healthy, or clean it up if it has become toxic. In this excerpt, a teacher ponders her school's climate and speculates on the forces that have created it.

The Withering of Curiosity

by Thomas French

Sometimes Mrs. Hay can almost see the neurons firing inside their brains. Like right now, as she talks about Ibsen. She tells them how old Henrik once said that the search for truth can make you lonely. She tells them how he said that the majority is never right until it does right. She even relates a little story about how the dear man used to keep a live scorpion—stinger and all—on his writing desk. It was a way of injecting venom into his plays.

"That's what he was doing," she says. "Getting out the venom."

When Mrs. Hay sits in front of a class like this one, bouncing ideas and questions off the kids, she looks so happy. If the whole school were filled with students like these, maybe she'd always be happy. Maybe she wouldn't worry so much about what's going to happen five or ten years down the line.

Mrs. Hay is not a doomsayer. She has taught at Largo High for two decades now, and she is proud of its record and accomplishments. But beneath the surface, something has gone wrong. It has been going wrong for years. Only now it's getting worse. Not just down in the pod, either.

To one degree or another, the same disease that is ravaging Mrs. Whitehead's sixth-period class—the apathy, the withering of curiosity, the almost palpable frustration and anger—already has infected the rest of Largo High, as it has infected so many other schools.

In some parts of the campus, it may be better hidden. It may not reveal itself so dramatically. But it's still there. It comes from outside. From all those thousands of TV screens, endlessly flickering through all those childhoods. From countless homes where no one talks to each other and where happiness is something that appears only on late-night reruns. From an entire society addicted to lottery tickets and get-rich schemes and miracle drugs and magical solutions and who knows how many other forms of instant gratification. The teachers don't particularly care where you put the blame. But they know it's out there, and for a long time now, they can't say exactly how long, it has been slipping into their schools—even schools such as Largo, where the walls in the front office are covered with awards and plaques and letters of commendation— and into every classroom.

The teachers talk about it. They stand in their empty rooms during their planning periods, when the kids are gone, and they talk about how scared they are.

"There *is* a problem," says Mrs. Hay.

They've got to get kids reading again. They have to find a way, she says, to make them understand that reading and writing and stretching their minds will eventually bring rewards that cannot be measured in dollars and cents. Somehow, she says, they have to show them that effort is its own reward.

STEVEN
AND JONATHAN

as presented by Elaine Landau

From *Teenagers Talk About School* by Elaine Landau. Copyright © 1988 by Julian Messner, an imprint of Silver Burdett Press, Simon and Schuster Elementary. Used by permission.

Since students are at the heart of education efforts, it is only reasonable to attend to their perspectives. Elaine Landau's compilation of student statements offers interesting insights into how some youngsters perceive school. If teachers are willing to solicit their own students' perspectives, they are likely to get observations that are as revealing and thought-provoking as these.

Steven and Jonathan

as presented by Elaine Landau

Steven

If a Martian landed on earth, and I had to advise him on how to get through an American junior high or high school, I think I'd quote the biblical saying "The meek shall inherit the earth." None of this Darth Vader or laser beam fancy stuff. Even someone from another planet could graduate if he just learned to show up on time, shut his mouth, and not make waves.

Most teachers like to have their sense of power and being in charge underscored. You have to stick to their rules even if they are obviously unfair. The teachers are the drill sergeants and we're the new recruits. You don't have to be smart to get a diploma. Mediocre will do, if you don't cause any trouble. The last thing a harried teacher wants is another irritation or a bothersome student. If you're not a discipline problem and you do the homework most of the time, you'll make it. Teachers like to feel that what they're doing is important. We're supposed to be the sponges—they're the water.

Our teachers may say that they long for bright, stimulating students, but when they're faced with classes of over thirty of us for five periods a day, they're grateful for the cheerful, polite, and orderly student, even if that person is intellectually dead. Killed by having successfully completed junior high, that person may be going through high school as a zombie.

Our vice principal is really authoritarian. If he were a storybook character he'd be the troll waiting under the bridge to devour a small child or perhaps a billy goat. He doesn't see us as young people with feelings. To him, kids are a sort of subspecies of the human race.

In fact, our whole school administration has no respect for the students' privacy or dignity. Once the vice principal had the janitor forcibly open a kid's locker because he suspected that the boy had a hidden stash of drugs there. Even though they rummaged through all the kid's personal stuff, they didn't find what they were looking for. The vice principal's suspicions had been off target, but nobody even apologized to the boy.

They hadn't needed a search warrant to do what they did. Yet, if the police did the same thing to them, they'd probably sue the cops in court for harassment or invasion of privacy or something like that.

Maybe we'd be better off if Martians did come to Earth and somehow gained control of our schools. At least there'd be new lesson plans. And maybe they'd bring a fresh approach to the classroom. Perhaps to them kids would just appear to be wrinkle-free young people, and not a subspecies of the human race.

Jonathan

One of the best courses I ever had in school was the English class I took last term. But I didn't feel that way about it from the start. Our teacher, Mr. Baker, was young and new at our school, and he ran the class in a way that was different from anything I've ever experienced. For example, on the first day of class he refused to tell us either what we'd be covering or what would be required of us. This made everyone feel a little nervous since a lot of those enrolled were honors students and extremely anxious about keeping up their grade point average.

The class was conducted as though it were a college seminar. Our desks were turned around to form a circle; we sat in class facing one another. Baker didn't lecture. Instead, he questioned us in a challenging and provocative manner. Our reactions to the various writers became the essence of the course. Mr. Baker usually added his opinion, but he made it clear that reading and enjoying literature was a subjective process and that there were no right or wrong answers—only personal interpretations. He used to say that each person brings as much to a book as the book brings to him.

You didn't take notes in Mr. Baker's class, which meant that you didn't know how to study for his tests. When we'd ask him what he wanted us to know, he'd say that he was interested only in what we thought about what we had read and our comparisons of the different texts covered.

At first it was hard not to feel uneasy about being unable to study for Mr. Baker's tests in the usual way.

A number of kids transferred to different English classes early on in the term. I stayed though, and now I'm really glad that I did. We did so many great things. Our class wasn't always held in the building. Sometimes Mr. Baker would get complimentary tickets to a local playhouse or he'd arrange for us to take part in a poetry festival.

Our final exam was unbelievable. There was only one question on it, and Mr. Baker gave it out to the class several weeks in advance of the test date. You could select any three works we studied and write one to two pages on each.

But it wasn't as easy as it sounds. Our papers could not contain the ideas that we had gone over in class. You had to think of something original. If you included one re-hashed idea in your exam booklet, you'd get an automatic C. For two repeated ideas or conclusions, you'd earn a D. If three or more of the ideas we had discussed in class were present on your paper, you'd be taking the course over in summer school.

At first I found Mr. Baker's requirement difficult, in fact, it seemed nearly impossible. After all, some of the smartest kids in the school were in that class, and hadn't they said every brilliant thing imaginable?

Apparently not. After years of being a student, for the first time I had to reach into my own mind to tap my creativity. I came up with a completely original paper, which I even enjoyed thinking about and writing.

Mr. Baker rewarded my efforts by giving me an A on my final. But actually he had done much more for me than that. Mr. Baker had forced us to think of him more as a guide than as an authority. We learned to develop our own thinking. He gave me the courage to accept and value my own interpretations.

Much of what Mr. Baker taught us could be applied to other school subjects as well as to some things in everyday life. It's a critical way of both viewing the world and learning to accept your own feelings. Some of us in his class feel grateful to Mr. Baker for conducting the class as he did. He helped us to lift all the boundaries set on our minds and our spirits—the same kinds of boundaries and pressures that so many of the other teachers use to confine us. Unfortunately, Mr. Baker is no longer at our school. There was some controversy over his refusal to teach the vocabulary lists deemed necessary for the SAT's by the English Department's head.

This year I'm back to studying vocabulary and taking complete sets of notes in my new English class. But what I'm doing now still hasn't wiped out all the good feelings that I came away with from Mr. Baker's class. I know that he made something wonderful happen to me and to most of the other students who stayed for the term. It was as if he freed a caged bird or untied a chained dog, and you don't easily forget a teacher like that.

TEACHING, LEARNING, AND THEIR COUNTERFEITS

by Mortimer Adler

From *Reforming Education: The Opening of the American Mind* by Mortimer Adler, edited by Geraldine Van Doren (New York: Collier Books, Macmillan Publishing Company, 1990). Copyright © 1976, 1987 by Mortimer Adler. Part of this essay also appeared in *From Parnassus*, edited by William R. Keylor and Dora B. Weiner (New York: Harper & Row, 1976). Used by permission of Mortimer Adler.

Mortimer Adler's achievements as an educator have stemmed from his drive to help students develop into reflective, thinking individuals. In 1940, with Robert Hutchins, he established the Great Books Foundation. He created and wrote the **Syntopican***, published in 1952, to accompany Encyclopedia Britannica's set of the Great Books of the Western World. With his publication of* **The Paideia Proposal** *in 1982, Adler argued for significant reform of K-12 education. In this essay, he expresses the ideas that are at the heart of that proposal.*

Teaching, Learning, and Their Counterfeits

by Mortimer Adler

Everyone knows, or certainly should know, that indoctrination is not genuine teaching and that the results of indoctrination are the very opposite of genuine learning. Yet, as a matter of fact, much that goes on in the classrooms of our schools is nothing but indoctrination. The results that are measured by our standardized tests are not products of genuine learning.

All learning is either by instruction or by discovery—that is, with or without the aid of teachers. The teachers who serve as instructors may be alive and in direct contact with those whom they instruct, as is always the case in classrooms or tutorials, or they may be present to the learner only in the form of books. The teacher who instructs by his writings cannot engage in discussion with those who are reading his works in order to learn; he can ask them initial questions, but he cannot ask any second questions—questions about answers they give to his initial questions. He is, therefore, seriously limited in his performance of the art of teaching, though he may have done what he could to apply the rules of that art in his effort to communicate what he knows.

That the effort to communicate what a man knows is not, *in itself,* effective teaching follows from the fact that such efforts are seldom if ever successful and, at best, they succeed only in part. Successful teaching occurs only when the mind of the learner passes from a state of ignorance or error to a state of knowledge. The knowledge acquired may be either something already known by the teacher, or something about which he himself is inquiring. In either case, the transformation effected in the mind of the learner is learning by instruction only if another human being has taken certain deliberate steps to bring about that transformation. What the teacher does must be deliberately calculated to change the mind of the learner. Merely motivating someone to learn is not enough; stimulation is not teaching.

Since whatever can be learned by instruction must necessarily have been learned first by discovery without the aid of teachers, it follows that teachers are, absolutely speaking, dispensable. Nevertheless, they are useful because most human beings need instruction to learn what they could have learned by discovering it for themselves. If we recognize, as we should, that genuine learning cannot occur without activity on the part of the learner (passive absorption or rote memorization does not deserve to be called learning), then we must also recognize that all learning is a process of discovery on the part of the learner.

This alters our understanding of the distinction between learning by discovery and learning by instruction. If the latter is not to be identified with passive absorption or rote memorization, then the distinction divides all active learning into two kinds—unaided discovery, discovery without the aid of teachers, on the one hand; and aided discovery, or discovery deliberately assisted by teachers, on the other. In both cases, the principal cause of learning is activity on the part of the learner engaged in the process of discovery; when instruction occurs, the teacher is at best only an instrumental cause operating to guide or facilitate the process of discovery on the part of the learner. To suppose that the teacher is ever more than an instrumental cause is to suppose that the activity of a teacher can by itself suffice to cause learning to occur in another person even though the latter remains entirely passive. This would view the learner as a patient being acted upon rather than as an agent whose activity is both primary and indispensable. In contrast, the instrumental activity of the teacher is always secondary and dispensable.

These basic insights are epitomized by Socrates when, in the *Theaetetus,* he describes his role as a teacher by analogy with the service performed by a midwife who does nothing more than assist the pregnant mother to give birth with less pain and more assurance. So, according to Socrates, the teacher assists the inquiring mind of the learner to give birth to knowledge, facilitating the process of discovery on the learner's part.

Teaching, like farming and healing, is a cooperative art. Understanding this, Comenius in *The Great Didactic* again and again compares the cultivation of the mind with the cultivation of the field; so, too, Plato compares the teacher's art with the physician's.

In arts such as shoemaking and shipbuilding, painting and sculpture (arts which I call "operative" to distinguish them from the three cooperative arts), the artist is the principal cause of the product produced. Nature may supply the materials to be fashioned or transformed, and may even supply models to imitate, but without the intervention of the artist's skill and causal efficacy, nature would not produce shoes, ships, paintings, or statues.

Unlike the operative artist, who aims either at beauty or utility, the cooperative artist merely helps nature to produce results that it is able to produce by its own powers, without the assistance of the artist—without the intervention of the artist's accessory causality. Fruits and grains grow naturally; the farmer intervenes merely to assure that these natural products grow with regularity and, perhaps, to increase their quantity. The body has the power to heal itself—to maintain health and regain health; the physician who adopts the Hippocratic conception of the healing art attempts to support and reinforce the natural processes of the body. The mind, like the body, has the power to achieve what is good for itself—knowledge and understanding. Learning would go on if there were no teachers, just as healing and growing would go on if there were no physicians and farmers.

Like the farmer and the physician, the teacher must be sensitive to the natural process that his art should help bring to its fullest fruition—the natural process of learning. It is the nature of human learning that determines the strategy and tactics of teaching. Since learning which results in expanded knowledge and improved understanding (rather than memorized facts) is essentially a process of discovery, the teacher's art consists largely in devices whereby one individual can help another to lift himself up from a state of knowing and understanding less to knowing and understanding more. Left to his own devices, the learner would not get very far unless he asked himself questions, perceived problems to be solved, suffered puzzlement over dilemmas, put himself under the necessity of following out the implications of this hypothesis or that, made observations and weighed the evidence for alternative hypotheses, and so on. The teacher, aware of these indispensable steps in the process by which he himself has moved his own mind up the ladder of learning, devises ways to help another individual engage in a similar process; and he applies them with sensitivity to the state of that other person's mind and with awareness of whatever special difficulties the other must overcome in order to make headway.

Discipline in the traditional liberal arts imparts the skills by which an individual becomes adept at learning. They are the arts of reading and writing, of speaking and listening, of observing, measuring, and calculating—the arts of grammar, rhetoric, and logic, the mathematical arts, and the arts of investigation. Without some proficiency in these arts, no one can learn very much, whether assisted or not by the use of books and the tutelage of teachers. Unless the teacher is himself a skilled learner, a master of the liberal arts which are the arts of learning, he cannot help those he attempts to teach acquire the skills of learning; nor can his superior skill in learning provide the learner with the help he needs in the process of discovery. The teacher must put himself sympathetically in the position of a learner who is less advanced than himself, less advanced both in skill and in knowledge or understanding. From that vantage point, he must somehow reenact—or simulate—for the learner the activities he himself engaged in to achieve his present state of mind.

The Hippocratic understanding of healing as a cooperative art provides us with analogical insights into the cooperative art of teaching. Hippocrates, whom we in the West regard as the father of medicine, wrote treatises setting forth the rules of healing as a cooperative art. They were rules for controlling the regimen of the patient—the food he ate, the air he breathed, his hours of waking and sleeping, the water he drank, the exercise he engaged in, and so forth. By controlling the patient's regimen—his diet, his hours, his activities, his environment—the physician helps the body to heal itself by its natural processes.

Administering drugs, introducing foreign substances into the body, Hippocrates regarded as the least cooperative of all medical treatments. Surgery he regarded as a drastic measure to be resorted to only when all cooperative methods failed; it was, strictly speaking, an *operative* rather than a *cooperative* procedure.

In the sphere of teaching, the analogue of surgery is indoctrination, the result of which is rote memorization, or some passive absorption of information without any understanding of it. Indoctrination does violence to the mind, as surgery does violence to the body, the only difference being that there is never any excuse for indoctrination, while there can be justification for surgery.

Teachers who regard themselves as the principal, even the sole, cause of the learning that occurs in their students simply do not understand teaching as a cooperative art. They think of themselves as producing knowledge or understanding in the minds of their students in the same way that shoemakers produce shoes out of pliable or plastic materials.

Only when teachers realize that the principal cause of the learning that occurs in a student is the activity of the student's own mind do they assume the role of cooperative artists. While the activity of the learner's mind is the principal cause of all learning, it is not the sole cause. Here the teacher steps in as a secondary and cooperative cause.

Just as, in the view of Hippocrates, surgery is a departure from healing as a cooperative art, so, in the view of Socrates, didactic teaching, or teaching by lecturing or telling rather than teaching by questioning and discussion, is a departure from teaching as a cooperative art.

Lecturing is that form of teaching which is analogous to the use of drugs and medication in the practice of medicine. No violence may be done to the mind if the lecturer eschews any attempt at indoctrination; but the lecture, even when it is attended to with maximum effort on the part of the auditor, is something that the mind must first absorb before it can begin to digest and assimilate what is thus taken in. If passively attended to and passively absorbed by the memory, the lecture has the same effect as indoctrination, even if the lecturer scrupulously intended to avoid that result. At its best, the lecture cannot be more than an occasion for learning, a challenge to the mind of the auditor, an invitation to inquiry. The lecture, in short, is no better than the book as a teacher—an oral rather than a written communication of knowledge.

If, however, the lecture is always accompanied by some discussion of whatever matters are didactically presented, if there is an active interchange between teacher and students through questioning, didactic teaching can, to some slight degree, become genuine teaching of knowledge understood instead of being an indoctrination of opinions to be committed to memory, retained, regurgitated on examinations, and then largely forgotten when the tests have been passed.

Analogous to the fully cooperative therapeutic technique of controlling the patient's regimen is the fully cooperative pedagogical technique of engaging the learner in discussion—teaching by asking instead of teaching by telling, asking questions not merely to elicit answers for the sake of grading them (as in a quiz session, which is not teaching at all), but asking questions that open up new avenues of inquiry.

When instruction is not accompanied by discovery, when instruction makes impressions on the memory with no act of understanding by the mind, then it is not genuine teaching, but mere indoctrination. Genuine teaching, in sharp distinction from indoctrination, always consists in activities on the part of teachers that cooperate with activities performed by the minds of students engaged in discovery.

The Greek word for mind, *nous,* identifies it with understanding. What we do not understand at all we retain solely through memory. Memory is a by-product of sense-perception; understanding, an act of the intellect. Statements that are verbally remembered and recalled should never be confused with facts understood.

Correlated with this distinction between mind and memory is the distinction between knowledge and opinion. To know something as opposed to holding a mere opinion about it is to understand it in the light of relevant reasons and supporting evidence.

Students acquire knowledge by the activity of their own minds, with or without the aid of teachers. How do they come by the opinions they hold, especially those acquired in the course of schooling?

They have adopted them on the naked authority of teachers who acted as if they were productive, not cooperative, artists—teachers who indoctrinated them by didactic instruction that was not accompanied by any acts of thinking or discovery on their part.

I have used the phrase "naked authority" to signify the authority teachers arrogate to themselves when they expect students to accept what they tell them simply because they are teachers. The only authority to which genuine teachers, as opposed to indoctrinators, should appeal is the authority of the relevant reasons or the evidence supporting whatever is to be learned. In the absence of such authority, teachers cannot help students acquire knowledge that is understood. They can only indoctrinate them with opinions they may or may not retain for long in their memories. Opinions adopted on the naked authority of teachers have little durability. Opinions remembered, with that memory reinforced temporarily by "boning up for tests," are opinions for the most part soon forgotten.

Much more durable are the habits of skill that are formed by the kind of teaching that is coaching, which is more cooperative than didactic teaching even when what is thus taught is illuminated by understanding through discussion. Habits are not memories. They can only be formed by coaching, never by lectures and the reading of textbooks.

Most students passing, at the end of one academic year, the standardized tests currently used, which are largely tests of memory, would probably not be able to pass them if they were given the same tests without warning at the beginning of the next academic year. But if the habitually possessed skills of students in reading and writing were measured by the level of their performance at the end of one academic year and then measured in the same way at a later time, little would be lost.

The understanding of ideas and knowledge understood, once acquired, has maximum durability. What is understood cannot be forgotten because it is a habit of the intellect, not something remembered. Anyone who comes to understand that a truth is self-evident only if it is undeniable because its opposite is unthinkable will understand it forever. To test or measure the understanding of students, the only effective instrument is an oral examination, a probing of the mind by persistent questioning that penetrates its depths as far as possible.

The misunderstanding of teaching and learning that prevails today has resulted in the deplorable fact, amply attested by Professor John Goodlad in *A Place Called School*, that 85 percent of all classroom time is consumed by unrelieved didactic teaching that is not genuine teaching at all, but sheer indoctrination. It results in the short-lived, mainly verbal, memory of mere opinions adopted on the naked authority assumed by indoctrinating teachers.

The conception of the teacher as one who has knowledge or information that he or she transmits to students as passive recipients violates the nature of teaching as a cooperative art. It assumes that genuine learning can occur simply by instruction, without acts of thinking and understanding that involve discovery by the minds of students.

The way in which we test or examine students and the way in which we grade them determines what teachers teach and how they teach, and what students learn and how they learn. Our present methods call for indoctrination rather than genuine teaching, and for memorizing rather than genuine learning.

Unless we radically change our present methods of testing and grading students, we cannot expect our teachers to become cooperative artists instead of mere indoctrinators, and we cannot expect our students to become genuine learners instead of mere memorizers.

All our written tests should be open-book examinations so that students prepare for them not by boning up on what they have not adequately remembered, but by trying to deepen their understanding of what they were taught, or sharpening their thinking about it. If habitual skills are to be evaluated, they should be tested by performances judged adequate or inadequate. And to measure levels of understanding, the only effective instrument is an oral examination.

Four things are needed in the training of teachers to make them cooperative artists:

WHAT'S WORTH KNOWING?

by Neil Postman and Charles Weingartner

From *Teaching as a Subversive Activity* by Neil Postman and Charles Weingartner (New York: Dell Publishing Company, 1969). Copyright © 1969 by Neil Postman and Charles Weingartner. Used by permission of Dell Books, a division of Bantam Doubleday Dell Publishing Group, Inc.

In their introduction to **Teaching As a Subversive Activity**, *Postman and Weingartner express one of their concerns with these words:*

School, after all, is the one institution in our society that is inflicted on everybody, and what happens in school makes a difference—for good or ill. We use the word "inflicted" because we believe that the way schools are currently conducted does very little, and quite probably nothing, to enhance the chances of mutual survival; that is, to help us solve any or even some of the problems we have mentioned. One way of representing the present condition of our educational system is as follows: It is as if we are driving a multimillion dollar sports car, screaming "Faster! Faster!" while peering fixedly into the rearview mirror. It is an awkward way to try to tell where we are, much less where we are going, and it has been sheer dumb luck that we have not smashed ourselves to bits—so far. We have paid almost exclusive attention to the car, equipping it with all sorts of fantastic gadgets and an engine that will propel it at ever greater speeds, but we seem to have forgotten where we wanted to go in it.

In this selection, the authors question the relevance of traditional school practices and suggest thoughtful alternatives. When the book was first published, it inspired many teachers to question and reshape their classroom practices. That it has the same effect on so many teachers today is a tribute to the authors' ever-relevant focus on preparing students to handle the upheaval and change that is such a marked feature of modern society.

What's Worth Knowing?

by Neil Postman and Charles Weingartner

Suppose all of the syllabi and curricula and textbooks in the schools disappeared. Suppose all of the standardized tests—city-wide, state-wide, and national—were lost. In other words, suppose that the most common material impeding innovation in the schools simply did not exist. Then suppose that you decided to turn this "catastrophe" into an opportunity to increase the relevance of the schools. What would you do?

We have a possibility for you to consider: suppose that you decide to have the entire "curriculum" consist of questions. These questions would have to be worth seeking answers to not only from your point of view but, more importantly, from the point of view of the students. In order to get still closer to reality, add the requirement that the questions must help the students to develop and internalize concepts that will help them to survive in the rapidly changing world of the present and future.

Obviously, we are asking you to suppose you were an educator living in the second half of the twentieth century. What questions would you have on your list?

Take a pencil and list your questions on the next page, which we have left blank for you. Please do not be concerned about defacing our book, unless, of course, one of your questions is going to be "What were some of the ways of earning a living in Ancient Egypt?" In that case, use your *own* paper.

Now, if one of your questions was something like "Why should you answer someone else's questions?," then you undoubtedly realize that we will submit our own sample list with some misgivings. As we have said, the ecology of the inquiry environment requires that the *students* play a central, but not necessarily exclusive, role in framing questions that they deem important. Even the most sensitive teacher cannot always project himself into the perspective of his students, and he dare not assume that *his* perception of reality is necessarily shared by them. With this limitation in mind, we can justify the list we will submit on several grounds. First, many of these questions *have* literally been asked by children and adolescents when they were permitted to respond freely to the challenge of "What's Worth Knowing?" Second, some of these questions are based on our careful *listening* to students, even though they were not at the time asking questions. Very often children make declarative statements about things when they really mean only to elicit an informative response. In some cases, they do this because they have learned from adults that it is "better" to pretend that you know than to admit that you don't. (An old aphorism describing this process goes: Children enter school as question marks and leave as periods.) In other cases, they do this because they do not know *how* to ask certain kinds of

questions. In any event, a simple translation of their declarative utterances will sometimes produce a great variety of deeply felt questions.

Our final justification rests with our own imagination. We have framed—as we asked you to do—some questions which, in our judgment, are responsive to the actual and immediate as against the fancied and future needs of learners in the world as it *is* (not as it *was*). In this, we have not surveyed thousands of students, but have consulted with many, mostly in junior and senior high school. We have tried variations of these questions with children in primary grades. By and large, the response was enthusiastic—and serious. There seemed to be little doubt that, from the point of view of the students, these questions made much more sense than the ones they usually have to memorize the right answers to in school. At this point it might be worth noting that our list of questions is intended to "educate" students. Contrary to conventional school practice, what that means is that we want to elicit from students the meanings that they have already stored up so that they may subject those meanings to a testing and verifying, reordering and reclassifying, modifying and extending process. In this process, the student is not a passive "recipient"; he becomes an active *producer* of knowledge. The word "educate" is closely related to the word "educe." In the oldest pedagogic sense of the term, this meant drawing out of a person something potential or latent. We can, after all, learn only in relation to what we already know. Again, contrary to common misconceptions, this means that, if we don't know very much, our capability for learning is not very great. This idea—

virtually by itself—requires a major revision in most of the metaphors that shape school policies and procedures.

Reflect on these questions—and others that these can generate. Please do not merely react to them.

What do you worry about most?

What are the causes of your worries?

Can any of your worries be eliminated? How?

Which of them might you deal with first? How do you decide?

Are there other people with the same problems? How do you know? How can you find out?

If you had an important idea that you wanted to let everyone (in the world) know about, how might you go about letting them know?

What bothers you most about adults? Why?

How do you want to be similar to or different from adults you know when you become an adult?

What, if anything, seems to you to be worth dying for?

How did you come to believe this?

What seems worth living for?

How did you come to believe this?

At the present moment, what would you most like to be—or be able to do? Why? What would you have to know in order to be able to do it? What would you have to do in order to get to know it?

How can you tell "good guys" from "bad guys"?

How can "good" be distinguished from "evil"?

What kind of a person would you most like to be? How might you get to be this kind of person?

At the present moment, what would you most like to be doing? Five years from now? Ten years from now? Why? What might you have to do to realize these hopes? What might you have to give up in order to do some or all of these things?

When you hear or read or observe something, how do you know what it means?

Where does meaning "come from"?

What does "meaning" mean?

How can you tell what something "is" or whether it is?

Where do words come from?

Where do symbols come from?

Why do symbols change?

Where does knowledge come from?

What do you think are some of man's most important ideas? Where did they come from? Why? How? Now what?

What's a "good idea"?

How do you know when a good or live idea becomes a bad or dead idea?

Which of man's ideas would we be better off forgetting? How do you decide?

What is "progress"?

What is "change"?

What are the most obvious causes of change? What are the least apparent? What conditions are necessary in order for change to occur?

What kinds of changes are going on right now? Which are important? How are they similar to or different from other changes that have occurred?

What are the relationships between new ideas and change?

Where do *new* ideas come from? How come? So what?

If you wanted to stop one of the changes going on now (pick one), how would you go about it? What consequences would you have to consider?

Of the important changes going on in our society, which should be encouraged and which resisted? Why? How?

What are the most important changes that have occurred in the past ten years? twenty years? fifty years? In the last year? In the last six months? Last month? What will be the most important changes next month? Next year? Next decade? How can you tell? So what?

What would you change if you could? How might you go about it? Of those changes which are going to occur, which would you stop if you could? Why? How? So what?

Who do you think has the most important things to say today? To whom? How? Why?

What are the dumbest and most dangerous ideas that are "popular" today? Why do you think so? Where did these ideas come from?

What are the conditions necessary for life to survive? Plants? Animals? Humans?

Which of these conditions are necessary for all life?

Which ones for plants? Which ones for animals? Which ones for humans?

What are the greatest threats to all forms of life? To plants? To animals? To humans?

What are some of the "strategies" living things use to survive? Which unique to plants? Which unique to animals? Which unique to humans?

What kinds of human survival strategies are (1) similar to those of animals and plants; (2) different from animals and plants?

What does man's language permit him to develop as survival strategies that animals cannot develop?

How might man's survival activities be different from what they are if he did not have language?

What other "languages" does man have besides those consisting of words?

What functions do these "languages" serve? Why and how do they originate? Can you invent a new one? How might you start?

What would happen, what difference would it make, what would man not be able to do if he had no number (mathematical) languages?

How many symbol systems does man have? How come? So what?

What are some good symbols? Some bad?

What good symbols could we use that we do not have?

What bad symbols do we have that we'd be better off without?

What's worth knowing? How do you decide? What are some ways to go about getting to know what's worth knowing?

It is necessary for us to say at once that these questions are not intended to represent a catechism for the new education. These are samples and illustrations of the kinds of questions we think worth answering. Our set of questions is best regarded as a metaphor of our sense of relevance. If you took the trouble to list your own questions, it is quite possible that you prefer many of them to ours. Good enough. The new education is a process and will not suffer from the applied imaginations of all who wish to be a part of it. But in evaluating your own questions, as well as ours, bear in mind that there are certain *standards* that must be used. These standards may also be stated in the form of questions:

Will your questions increase the learner's *will* as well as his capacity to learn?

Will they help to give him a sense of joy in learning?

Will they help to provide the learner with confidence in his ability to learn?

In order to get answers, will the learner be required to make inquiries? (Ask further questions, clarify terms, make observations, classify data, etc.?)

Does each question allow for alternative answers (which implies alternative modes of inquiry)?

Will the process of answering the questions tend to stress the uniqueness of the learner?

Would the questions produce different answers if asked at different stages of the learner's development?

Will the answers help the learner to sense and understand the universals in the human condition and so enhance his ability to draw closer to other people?

If the answers to these questions about your list of questions are all "yes," then you are to be congratulated for insisting upon extremely high standards in education. If that seems an unusual compliment, it is only because we have all become accustomed to a conception and a hierarchy of standards that, in our opinion, is simultaneously upside-down and irrelevant. We usually think of a curriculum as having high standards if "it" covers ground, requires much and difficult reading, demands many papers, and if the students for whom it is intended do not easily get "good" grades. Advocates of "high standards" characteristically and unwittingly invoke other revealing metaphors. One of the most frequently used of these is "basic fundamentals." The most strident advocates of "high, and ever yet higher, standards" insist that these be "applied" particularly to "basic fundamentals." Indulging our propensity to inquire into the language of education, we find that the essential portion of the word "fundamentals" is the word "fundament." It strikes us as poetically appropriate that "fundament" also means the buttocks, and specifically the anus. We will resist the temptation to explore the unconscious motives of "fundamentalists." But we cannot resist saying that their "high standards" represent the *lowest possible standards imaginable* in any conception of a new education. In fact, so low, that the up-down metaphor is not very useful in describing it.

What one needs to ask of a standard is not, "Is it high or low?," but, "Is it appropriate to your goals?" If your goals are to make people more alike, to prepare them to be docile functionaries in some bureaucracy, and to prevent them from being vigorous, self-directed learners, then the standards of most schools are neither high nor low. They are simply apt. If the goals are those of a new education, one needs standards based on the actual activities of competent, confident learners when they are genuinely engaged in learning. One must be centrally concerned with the hearts and minds of learners—in contrast to those merely concerned with the "fundament." No competent learner ever says to himself, "In trying to solve this problem, I will read two books (not less than 30 pages from each). Then, I will make a report of not less than 20 pages, with a minimum of 15 footnotes...." The only place one finds such "standards" is in a school syllabus. *They do not exist in natural, human learning situations, since they have nothing to do with the conditions of learning—with what the learner needs to be and to do in order to learn about learning, or indeed about anything.* Any talk about high standards from teachers or school administrators is nonsense unless they are talking about *standards of learning* (as distinct from standards for grading, which is what is usually meant). What this means is that there is a need for a new— and "higher"—conception of "fundamentals." Everyone, at present, is in favor of having students learn the fundamentals. For most people, "the three R's," or some variation of them, represent what is fundamental to a learner. However, if one *observes* a learner and asks himself, "What is it that this organism needs without which he cannot thrive?," it is impossible to come up with the answer "The three R's." The "new fundamentals" derive from the emotional and intellectual realities of the human condition, and so "new" answers (well beyond the three-R's type) are possible in response to the question. In *In Defense of Youth,* Earl Kelley lists five such possible answers:

1. the need for other people
2. the need for good communication with other people
3. the need for a loving relationship with other people
4. the need for a workable concept of self
5. the need for freedom.

One does not need to accept all of these in order to accept Kelley's *perspective* on what is fundamental. Obviously, we would want to add to his list "the need to know how to learn," as well as some others which are suggested by our list of "standards" questions. The point is that any curriculum that does not provide for needs as viewed from this perspective—"What does the organism require in order to thrive?"—is not, by our definition, concerned with "fundamentals."

We would like to invite you now to reexamine our sample questions. They represent, after all, a possible curriculum for the new education: The What's-Worth-Knowing Questions Curriculum. This curriculum has several characteristics that require elaboration here. For example, note that all the questions are of a divergent, or open-ended, nature and that each one demands that the learner narrow its focus. Part of the process of learning how to learn is the rephrasing, refining, and dividing of a "worth knowing" question into a series of "answerable worth-knowing questions." It is a fact not easily learned (and almost never in school) that the "answer" to a great many questions is "merely" another question. This is not only true of such questions as we have listed, but even of such questions as "What is a noun?," "Who discovered oxygen?," and "What is the principal river of Uruguay?"

HOW OUR SCHOOLS COULD BE

by Deborah Meier

From *Phi Delta Kappan* Vol. 76, No. 5 (January 1995) pages 369-373. Reprinted with permission from *Phi Delta Kappan*.

Deborah Meier, now at the Annenberg Institute, was a principal in New York City and the director of the Central Park East schools. In this essay, she proposes reforms by describing what she and others did to improve the school experience for the children of District 4.

How Our Schools Could Be

by Deborah Meier

We stand poised between two alternative visions of the schools of tomorrow. The tough part is that these two visions are often espoused by the same people, and teachers and citizens alike are led to believe that both can be carried out simultaneously. In fact, they stand in chilling contrast to each other.

One vision rests on the assumption that top-down support for bottom-up change—which everyone is rhetorically for—means that the top does the critical intellectual work, defining purposes and content as well as how to measure them, and the bottom does the "nuts and bolts," the "how-to"—a sort of "men's work" versus "women's work" division of labor.

The second vision rests on a different assumption—that the only top-down reforms that are useful are those that help to create and sustain self-governing learning communities. When schools see themselves as membership communities, not service organizations, parents and teachers discuss ideas, argue about purposes, and exercise judgment, because taking responsibility for making important decisions is at the heart of what it means to be well-educated.

Students can't learn unless the adults who must show them the way practice what they preach.

The Goals 2000 national education agenda, with its focus on setting measurable goals and standards, is weighted down with assumptions that the top does the critical intellectual work and the bottom is left with doing the how-to. But that second camp, with its alternative assumptions of what schools could be, is showing a surprising capacity to thrive these days. At least for a time. I've been told that I'm ignoring the train that's already left the station and is coming down the line, the "do-it-or-else" express. But if history is any guide, such fast-track solutions often turn out to be expensive dead ends.

Can we post a counter-mandate to the "all students will" dicta being invented by expert, university-based task forces? Let me propose a mandate saying, "Standards shall be phased in only as fast as the school, the district, and the state can bring their adult staff members up to the standards they expect of all 18-year-old students." That might delay the train just a little.

We in New York have historically lived under the imposition of an awesome array of local and state curricular mandates and outcomes assessments. (Except for private schools, which were always free to ignore them and always have.) Every so often someone gets the idea to create still another set, generally laid right on top of the old ones, and then moves on to other things. New York teachers are experienced and inventive saboteurs of the best and worst of such plans. Our state is home therefore to some of the greatest as well as some of the worst of schools.

But the second alternative described above is staring us in the face. And it is gathering surprising national momentum, even from such unexpected (for old cynics like me) places as the New York State Board of Regents (New York's state board of education). The state authorities are now embarked on a new and more promising approach, as are the governor, the mayor, and the local New York City board of education—despite contradictions all over the place. That so many are now marching to a different drummer in the name of a different vision of "systemic" reform is heartening. This different vision has the support this time around not only of child-centered romantics like me, but also of hardheaded corporate and management reformers, such as the folks who invented the team approach to building the Saturn car or the Deming way of managing businesses.

We also have some hardheaded history of school reform to point to, on a scale that should make it hard to dismiss this "other" way as suitable only for the brave and the foolish, the maverick and the exceptional. It's no longer "alternative," but almost mainstream.

When a handful of like-minded teachers in East Harlem's Community School District No. 4 started a "progressive, open education" elementary school, Central Park East, in 1974, we were encouraged, by the then district superintendent, Anthony Alvarado, to pay little heed to rules and regulations. We were told to create the kind of school we believed would work for the children of District 4. This revolutionary autonomy, which in local circles was referred to alternatively as "creative compliance" and "creative noncompliance," was simply a public and collaborative version of what many of us had long done behind closed doors.

Central Park East, along with more than 30 other small schools of choice begun by District 4 during the next 10 years, was and remains an amazing success story. We lived a somewhat lonely existence for a decade, but today both the Central Park East schools and the District 4 "way" have been roughly replicated in dozens of New York City school districts and are now part of accepted citywide reform plans. What the schools that have adopted this model share is a way of looking at children that is reminiscent of good kindergarten practice. Or, put another way, they operate according to what we know about how human beings learn, and they are guided by a deep-seated respect for all the parties involved—parents, teachers, and students.

Kindergarten is the one place—for many children it may be the last place—where such mutual respect has been a traditional norm (if not always practiced). A kindergarten teacher, for example, is expected to know children well, even if they don't hand in their homework, finish their Friday tests, or pay attention. Kindergarten teachers know that learning must be personalized, because kids come that way—no two alike. They know that parents and the community must be partners, or kids will be shortchanged. Kindergarten teachers know that part of their job description is to help children learn to become more self-reliant— starting with tying their shoes and going to the bathroom on their own.

Alas, it is the last time that children are given such independence, that they are encouraged to make choices and allowed to move about on their own. Having learned to use the bathroom by themselves at age 5, at age 6 they're required to wait until the whole class lines up at bathroom time. In kindergarten, parents and teachers meet to talk and often have one another's phone numbers. After that, communication is mainly one-way and impersonal. In kindergarten, we design our rooms for real work, not just passive listening. We put things in the room that we have reason to believe will appeal to children, things that will grab their interests and engage their minds and hearts. The older that children get, the less we take into account the importance of their own interests, their own active learning. In kindergarten, teachers are editors, critics, cheerleaders, and caretakers, not just lecturers or deliverers of instruction. What Theodore Sizer calls "coaching" is second nature to the kindergarten teacher, who takes for granted that her job description includes curriculum development as well as ongoing assessment.

But what's true for students is also true for teachers: they have less and less authority, responsibility, and independence as their charges get older—until, of course, the students make it into college or graduate school. Then both teachers and students go back to kindergarten.

It was Sizer who, when he came to visit our school, pointed out to us that the kindergarten principles of Central Park East were the same principles he was espousing for the nation's high schools. He suggested that we start a secondary school, beginning with seventh-graders, as a continuation of our elementary school. It was 1984—the right moment for such an idea. And even though community school districts in New York City are not supposed to operate high schools, the idea was approved. Central Park East would just keep going from kindergarten through the 12th grade.

So we made the decision to see if we could use the principles of a good kindergarten as the basis for running a good high school. We opened Central Park East Secondary School in 1985 with a seventh grade and grew one grade a year each year thereafter.

We were not without great trepidation. Running through our minds were thoughts such as: Dare we? Could we take on teenagers? Aren't teenagers impossible to handle? I had spent a lot of years avoiding adolescents in groups of more than two, and I realized that it would be hard to build a secondary school without bumping into them in groups of at least three. We also knew that high school kids wouldn't like to be compared to kindergartners—or even sixth-graders. We needed to create new rituals that symbolized their new maturity. Finally, we were aware that, as the school was "growing up," it meant that we needed to be concerned about the expectations at the other end—what colleges and employers might want. Was there such a thing as being too nurturing or giving kids too much independence and too great a sense of empowerment?

One thing we very much wanted was to get away from the contemporary mode of breaking everything down into discrete bits and pieces—whether subject matter or "thinking skills." We were determined to keep intact the elementary school tradition of respect for the wholeness of both subject matter and human learning. We were looking for ways to build a school that offered youngsters a deep and rich curriculum that would inspire them with the desire to know more—that would cause them to fall in love with books and with stories of the past, that would instill in them a sense of wonder at how much there is to learn.

We also saw schools as models of the possibilities of democratic life. Although students' classroom lives could certainly be made more democratic than traditional schools encouraged, we saw it as equally important that the school lives of *adults* be made more democratic. It seemed unlikely that we could foster democratic values in our school unless the adults had significant rights within their workplace. We wanted not just good individual classrooms but a good school.

Another priority for us was creating a setting in which all members of the community were expected to engage in the discussion of ideas and in the "having of their own wonderful ideas," as Eleanor Duckworth has put it. Indeed, one of our most prominently stated, up-front aims was the cultivation of what we came to call "Habits of Mind"—habits that apply to all academic and nonacademic subject matter and to all thoughtful human activities. The five we came up with are not exhaustive, but they suggest the kinds of questions that we believed a well-educated person raises about his or her world.

- How do we know what we think we know? What's our evidence? How credible is it?
- Whose viewpoint are we hearing, reading, seeing? What other viewpoints might there be if we changed our position—our perspective?
- How is one thing connected to another? Is there a pattern here?
- How else might it have been? What if? Supposing that?
- What difference does it make? Who cares?

In order to carry out our basic mission of teaching students to use their minds well and preparing them to live productive, socially useful, and personally satisfying lives, we approach curriculum with these habits as the backdrop and specific "essential" questions at the core. Clearly, we can't depend on textbooks. Many courses don't use them at all, except perhaps as reference books. We cover less and, we hope, uncover a lot more. We integrate different academic disciplines—history with literature, science with math. In the jargon of the Coalition of Essential Schools, this is the "less is more" principle. We spend, for example, two years on biology, mostly focused on a few central biological issues, and two years on American history—and we don't pretend to cover it.

We do more "hands-on" experimental work. We expect kids to read many different sources on the same subject, to use the library a lot, to write a lot (preferably on a computer), and to think and discuss their ideas with many different people. We expect them to share their knowledge with one another and to work in groups as well as on their own. Our curriculum is designed to reinforce the connection between "school" knowledge and "real world" knowledge and to include multiple perspectives.

Most of our students do take most of the standard city and state competency tests, and we provide coaching for such tests, as well as for the SAT. But we don't see these tests as a measuring rod. They capture neither essential intellectual competence nor the demonstrated capacity of our students to use their knowledge, to care for others, to imagine how others think and feel, and to be prepared to speak up and be heard. These skills are no less critical, no less rigorous. They are part of the "hard" stuff.

Twenty years of documented evidence—regarding high school graduation, drop-out rates, and college acceptances, for example—are hard to dispute. The Central Park East schools are demonstrably successful. Over 90% of the graduates of the elementary school go on to earn high school diplomas, and 90% of those who enter the high school not only receive high school diplomas but go on to college— nearly double the rate for the city as a whole. Furthermore, it is hard to attribute our remarkable statistics to having selected an elite or favored group. The student body of both the elementary and the high schools has always been about 40% Hispanic, 45% African American, and 15% other (Asian and white). Over two-thirds are poor enough to be eligible for free or reduced-price lunches, and at least 20% are labeled as "special ed" or "handicapped." They come to us looking remarkably like the assortment of students in the city as a whole. They leave, however, with substantially greater life choices.

But, proud as we are of these schools, we do not see what we do as the "best or only way" to educate children. As Seymour Fliegel, a former deputy superintendent in District 4, has put it, "The aim here has been to create a system that—instead of trying to fit all students into some standardized school—has a school to fit every student in this district. No kid gets left out, no kid gets lost. Every kid is important, every kid can learn if you put him or her in the right environment. But since kids have this huge range of different needs, different interests, and different ways of learning, we've got to have a wide diversity of schools."

While it has taken time for the District 4 ideas to catch on and for Central Park East's particular approach to spread, today both are "in the mainstream." Everyone is imitating the system of choice used in District 4, and there are more than 50 small public schools in New York City created in this tradition. Plans are afoot to vastly increase this number over the next five years. There are also plans to introduce innovations that will better match these new, less standardized approaches to teaching and learning with the ways in which we hold schools accountable.

It is clear that choice plans will require creative revisions in our current rules and regulations. As schools develop a variety of obviously different solutions, it will not be possible to assign students to schools by street address or lottery. Parents and children will have to be involved in making choices about which school they think will best suit the student's needs, talents and interests. Eventually all school districts may wish to develop schools of choice, even as they may also (as in District 4) give priority to parents on the basis of residence. Another way of lessening the transportation problems that are inherent in many choice plans is to locate several small schools in the same building.

The crucial decision inside in the District 4 "revolution" of two decades ago was to create a broad and diverse set of new schools, not to reform existing schools. This meant that the district could focus on encouraging schoolpeople to innovate, instead of on monitoring them for compliance with district-mandated reforms. The next phase will do well not to ignore the lessons learned: it's easier to design a new school culture than to change an existing one.

And it's the *whole* school culture—not this or that program—that stands in the way of learning.

The role of parents in the new schools was another central issue. Choice offered a way of providing for increased professional decision making without pitting parents and teachers against one another in a useless power struggle. Furthermore, small schools of choice offered everyone—teachers and families—vastly more time to meet together and work out differences through both formal and informal structures. The time needed is considerable but worth it. One top-down mandate we'd have no trouble with would be legislation requiring employers to provide time off for parents to attend school meetings.

Indeed, no school can complete its educational task without the support and trust of a student's family. Such trust rests on mutual respect and is never a luxury. Without it, the schools are crippled—and all the more so where differences in race, religion, and language between school staff and community are greatest. Young people sent to school with a message of distrust for the motives and methods of the school are fighting an uphill battle. They are always warily looking for hidden traps. And they will find plenty of them, since teachers too often don't hear the mixed messages they send out regarding their respect for children's families and communities.

Teachers rate "parental indifference" as their number-one complaint. That's a misreading of what keeps parents and teachers apart. Unless and until the two groups feel able to join together as advocates for the common good of youngsters, such apparent "indifference" will remain. We will not create serious educational breakthroughs until we can meet as allies.

Schoolpeople must learn to share with parents some of the autonomy associated with what are now being called "charter" schools: the control over administrative, curricular, staffing, and fiscal matters that allows them to pursue their own special approach to the education of children and young people.

We need such small autonomous schools so that democratic governance systems become possible—so that it doesn't seem silly to talk of "everyone" getting together. Just as the Empire State Building contains dozens of companies, so our big school buildings could contain many schools. They could contain schools, furthermore, serving different age groups. They might hire a building manager to deal solely with building matters, as the Empire State Building does. But the educational life of each school would remain distinct and independent. Simple changes that are impossible to make in a mega-school can be decided in one afternoon and implemented the next morning in a small school. You can even dispense with all permanent committees and representative bodies if you get your numbers right. It's our guess that a few hundred students with a faculty of under 20 is about optimum size for effective, democratic schooling. (Those figures don't preclude a half dozen or more schools in one building.)

Teachers will not have a major impact on the way students use their minds until teachers come to know how their students' minds are working—one by one. Teachers cannot help young people make sense of things if they do not have time to answer their students' questions—and time to really hear the questions. They cannot improve a student's writing if there isn't time to read it, reflect on it, and then occasionally meet with the student to talk it over together. They cannot find ways to connect new ideas with old ones if they have no control over curriculum or pacing. Nor can they influence the values and aspirations of young people if they cannot shape the tone and value system of their classrooms and schools.

But what about the loud cries for "accountability" that play such a major role in the support of top-down schemes? Who will tell us if it's "world class"? How will we know for sure how students stack up against one another nationally and internationally in the great race to see who's first?

Small, self-governed schools are at an advantage when it comes to being accountable to their own *immediate* community—parents, students, and fellow staff members. But we need to turn our attention to the question of how schools that set out to be independent and idiosyncratic can meet the legitimate demands for broader accountability to taxpayers. We've built our current system of public accountability on the basis of the factory-model school with its interchangeable parts. It's no wonder that we get almost no useful or honest information back. The task that lies ahead of us is to respond to democratically established norms for equity, access, outcomes, and fiscal integrity without sacrificing our educational principles. Given that few if any of these legitimate needs are currently being met, we need not expect a miracle answer as we design our better mousetraps. We're not catching any mice now. But that doesn't mean that mousetraps are not needed.

The danger here is that we will cramp the needed innovations with overambitious demands for accountability. Practical realism must prevail. Changes in the daily conduct of schooling—whether they relate to new curriculum or pedagogy or just to new ways of collaborating and governing—are hard, slow, and above all immensely time-consuming; they require a level of trust and patience that goes beyond that to which we are accustomed.

The structural reforms—changes in size, the role of choice, and shifts in power relationships—may be hard to make. But to some degree these are the changes that can be "imposed" from above. The trouble is that they merely lay the foundation for the slow and steady work that will have an actual impact on young people's intellectual and moral development. That's the tough realization. Some claim we can't afford such slow changes. They are wrong. There is nothing faster. If we try to go faster we may get somewhere faster—but not where we need to go.

Vandalism, assault, truancy, and apathy on the part of students cannot be eliminated by more of the same—metal detectors, identification cards, automated lateness calls, automatic expulsions and holdovers. Instead, these ills require an assault by schoolpeople on the culture of anonymity that permeates youngsters lives. Our children need stable personal relationships more than ever, and our schools offer such relationships less than ever.

Although the reasons for the current national concern about schooling may have little to do with democracy, the reforms described here have everything to do with it. Giving wider choices and more power to those who are closest to the classroom are not reforms that appeal to busy legislators, politicians, and central board officials. Such reforms seem too messy and too hard to track. They cannot be initiated on Monday and measured on Friday. They require fewer constraints, fewer rules—not more of them. They require asking why it matters and who cares—not lists of 465 skills, facts, and concepts multiplied by the number of disciplines academia can invent. They require initiating a debate in this nation that might shake us to the roots, a debate about what we value so dearly that we incarcerate our children for 12 years to make sure they've "got it." There *has* to be a better reason than to house them while we're busy, to keep them from taking our jobs, or merely to socialize them into packs or sort them into their proper pecking order.

A democratic society has a right to insist that the central function of schooling is to cultivate the mental and moral habits that a modern democracy requires. These include openness to other viewpoints, the capacity to sustain uncertainty, the ability to act on partial knowledge, and the inclination to step into the shoes of others—all habits that can be uncomfortable to have but, it is hoped, hard to shake. Until we face the fundamental question of the purpose of schooling, it makes little sense to keep asking for better tools to measure what we haven't agreed about. "What's it for?" the young ask often enough. It's time adults took the question seriously. There are no silver bullets when it comes to raising children right, no fast-track solutions with guaranteed cures. The only sensible course involves hard work, keeping your eyes on the prize, and lots of patience for the disagreements that inevitably arise.

THE FUTURE OF SCHOOLS AND HOW TO GET THERE FROM HERE

by R.G. Des Dixon

From *Phi Delta Kappan* Vol. 75, No. 5 (January 1994) pages 360-65. Reprinted with permission from *Phi Delta Kappan*.

R. G. Des Dixon was in charge of curriculum and professional development for the Ontario (Canada) Teachers' Federation and is currently an education analyst who lives near Toronto. In this essay he proposes reforms that go far beyond the usual suggestions for improving education.

The Future of Schools and How to Get There from Here

by R.G. Des Dixon

In the summer of 1992 I received a phone call from Theodore Sizer. He told me that my new book, *Future Schools,* is important and should be taken seriously. Elation at my end. But he also said that he hadn't had time to read my 500 pages closely enough to write critical comments. Disappointment at my end.

Something about that elation-to-disappointment sequence rang a forgotten bell in my mind. When the memory operator finally connected my mental line, I remembered a call some 33 years before—in November 1959. The *Kappan* had just planted the seed that grew into *Future Schools* by publishing my article "Are Principals Obsolete?" In it I proposed replacing principals with committees called "Adcoms," which are essentially governing committees composed of elected representatives of the teachers, students, and community.

My phone rang that long-ago November, and a professor at Columbia told me that he had read the *Kappan* article and thought my concept an important one that had to be taken seriously. Elation at my end. But he also said that he doubted anyone was ready for it. Disappointment at my end.

For years responses to that *Kappan* article have trickled in from far and wide, all more or less positive. In 1969, a decade after its publication, I received a letter asking whether any schools in Canada or the U.S. had the Adcom arrangement in place. My answer was no in 1969.

But I remain hopeful for 1999 or 2009. Metropolitan Miami, Chicago, and a few other places are inching in the right direction—even if they haven't yet got a clear picture of the whole road that leads to good schools. Their problem is the same one that confounded my 1959 proposal, the same one that plagues Sizer's Coalition of Essential Schools, the same one that has bedeviled all education reformers since Dewey: the changes proposed are too narrowly conceived to kill off the old model of schooling, so it eventually kills or cripples them.

The school as an organism routinely accepts cosmetic changes and even a bit of plastic surgery now and then for the sake of appearances. But it hemorrhages away transfusions of fresh blood and rejects transplants for its diseased vital organs. It remains forever alive on life-support systems, even though it is brain dead. If we want to change the school significantly, we must smother it with a critical mass of changes in rapid succession.

A "critical mass" implies so many changes as to constitute a new model of schooling. Unfortunately, nobody has the specs for such an entirely new model. Academics and innovators have been too busy with patches for the old model. Year in, year out, the education industry offers the public Band-Aids for whatever school wound is suppurating at the moment.

Meanwhile, other industries always have new models in the wind tunnel. Purveyors of everything from cars to computers flaunt their new feathers in a mating dance intended to whip up the public appetite in time for the consummation. It's called creating market readiness. But the education industry has no new feathers, so we can't dance.

Critics of my *Kappan* article never suggested whole new models. Educators don't typically think that way. Instead, they complained that changing the principal's office wouldn't change the classroom. So I proposed a different classroom method, an improvement on the concept of open education. The critics then lamented that changing classroom methods wouldn't change teacher education to match. So I came up with a different kind of teacher training, rather like the studio method of training actors. Critics said that wouldn't make any difference, because it wouldn't change teachers already in the schools. So I distinguished between personal and corporate professional development and said that the latter was synonymous with curriculum implementation and was therefore a responsibility of government that must be built into the regular school day of every teacher. The critics murmured.... But you get the picture. I kept stepping back further and further to include more in my field of vision and revision.

Meanwhile, I began searching the world for a better model of schooling. I began my quest with a 233-page comparison of schools in the U.S. and Canada. I found them to be twins. So I kept searching. I studied schools in more than a hundred countries and found them to be first cousins sharing similar genetic defects. Local cultures may have marginally modified the ubiquitous model, but I saw that I could set up shop as a teacher anywhere in the world on five minutes' notice. Schools are that much alike.

On a scale of 1 to 10, schools in all the developed countries rate about a 3.5. If a country is better at one thing, it is weaker at another. And nearly all countries are doing the wrong things better than ever. Worldwide, school is a pufferbelly locomotive chugging incongruously through a high-tech landscape, spewing human soot.

With the whole world in my field of vision, I felt that I was floating somewhere in space, watching the schools spin into oblivion. From that lonely distance I saw something that I had not seen up close: the model of schooling and the model of childhood are Siamese twins sharing the same central nervous system; if one is hurt, the other flinches. Thus you can't treat one and not the other.

From that moment, *Future Schools* began to take shape, a whole new model of schooling and a matching new model of childhood. Our current models of schooling and childhood are of recent origin—only about 600 years old in the 6,000-year history of civilization—and they grew up together influencing each other. Until this century, the model of schooling actually led the model of childhood. Special clothes for children, the separation of children from adults, the ideal of childhood as a time of innocence, punishment used for purification and control, lock-step restrictions on child development—so many characteristics—came to the model of childhood from the model of schooling. Now, in the 1990s, the *reality* of childhood (but not the sentimental model) is changing so fast that it is well in front of the model of schooling.

More than anything else, it was direct access to information that allowed childhood to sprint past schooling and get out in front: first mass-market print, then movies, then radio, then television, now computers. But dozens of other momentous changes speeded the redefinition of childhood in this century: wars, mass migrations, changes in the status of women and minorities, the population explosion, family breakdown, democratization of institutions other than schools, cycles of boom and bust, and so on.

Taken together, a combination of 20th-century circumstances that affect the young constitutes a major—but barely acknowledged—change in society. Neither the media nor our opinion leaders have noticed that children themselves are redefining childhood. The very young consume all types of information via television and computers, while our model of childhood still views them as ignorant and innocent. Teens spend most of their time working for pay, listening to music, and watching television, but the model still pretends that school is their primary activity. They are indispensable to such major industries as fast food, supermarkets, gas stations, retail stores, and hospitals, but the model sees them as outside the labor force. They are looking after themselves and running households for absentee adults, but the model sees them as helpless. They are sexually active, while the sentimental model of childhood says they are nonsexual.

At this moment, millions of high school students are working 55 hours a week or more, when school, home, and paid hours are totaled. But nobody has bothered to create (let alone accept and control) a "total job description" for students that matches the reality of their lives, including school, extracurricular activities, homework, after-hours jobs, household chores, and so on. Children are the most exploited, overworked, and underpaid class in society.

None of the following realities matches the 1940-ish Andy Hardy image of childhood to which society so fervently clings. Children—not old people or women or any racial group—are the poorest members of society. Yet significant numbers of children in their teens attend universities, graduate, and go on to become physicians, engineers, scientists, and mathematicians. Most male and female prostitutes begin working regularly at 16 or younger, and many street-level drug dealers are children. Children are the last visible minority without human rights. For over a decade boys of 12 to 16 years of age have been fighting in Eritrea, Sudan, Somalia, Israel (in the Intifada), Iraq, Iran, South Africa, Nicaragua, and other countries. Political candidates routinely say that junior high school audiences are among the best informed about issues in federal and state elections.

Our model of childhood dictates that children be passive instead of active, incapable instead of capable, directed instead of self-directed, acquiescent instead of assertive, dependent rather than independent. We have Mickey Moused the lives of children in schools by denying them control, the very thing we should be teaching them so that they can find meaning in life and learn to survive in the real world of childhood. Instead of validating the new self-reliance that is the essence of their reality in the community, schools treat teens as recidivist ring-around-a-rosiers even though, when they're out of school, they may have lovers, drive cars, and work for a living. The young express their frustration by dropping out, smoking, taking drugs, getting pregnant, forming gangs, and committing violent acts.

Our response to their expressed frustration is to set up committees of adults, build more sports facilities to be run by adults, provide more courses to be taught by adults, and improve consultation with parents, who cannot be changed in time to save any current generation of children. Except for a few activists for children's rights, our leading thinkers never set about creating a new model of childhood that matches reality. Instead, we sing praise to the sentimental model of childhood that, as a social convention, parallels 19th-century foot-binding in China. Both conventions require constant restriction, retard growth, subjugate a large minority, deform for life, and are thought by the perpetrators to be beautiful.

As deliberately as the old model disempowers children, the model I propose in *Future Schools* seeks to empower them. The new model accommodates the new realities of childhood that already exist and simultaneously reclaims for education its historic place as a leader in the development of models of childhood and schooling. For that last reason alone, teachers should be the eager leaders in community discussions that establish new models in the public mind. All the great opportunities for teachers lie in their assuming such leadership. If they fail, corporate giants in telecommunications will assume leadership. The Edison

Project of Whittle Communications will then point the way.

Student government has never been taken seriously by school reformers, but it must be central to any new model of schooling. By developing strong and relevant student government, schools will fulfill their long-neglected obligation to teach the democratic process and at the same time will provide sane leadership for society in its inevitable move toward children's rights. The test of student government is this: Is there anything being managed by school or district officials that could be managed by student government? If so, student government is not functioning properly.

In the new model, all school rules issue from and are enforced by student government and its committees. Parents, politicians, administrators, and teachers encourage student governments and student media to deal forthrightly and in-depth with the very matters that are now being censored: sex, politics, social issues, values, trends, children's rights, the re-definition of childhood, and so on. Student governments act as labor unions to promote and protect the interests of students in the part-time job market. If they are thoroughly trained, student governments can be valuable evaluators of all aspects of schooling, including curricula and teachers. In a reconstituted student government, service on the student council is a top-priority learning activity; thus student council meetings must take place during the school day, and office holders must receive academic credit for serving.

In the classroom, my proposed model requires a kind of teacher that has never before existed; I use the name *hi* (plural *hies)*—an abbreviation of human interactor—to convey their new role. And to describe the room in which that role is played, I prefer not to use the term *classroom* (since classes in the conventional sense are rarely taught there except in the early grades), but to call it instead a *living room.* In the new model, children of all ages, from preschoolers to 18-year-olds, spend about three years in each living room before moving on to the next, so that every child experiences six living rooms before graduation.

Very young children spend most of the day in the living room, but, as students grow older, they make increasing use of other rooms. The living room is home base, and every student keeps returning to it (or checking in by phone or computer when on learning missions outside the school). The hi knows when and why students leave the living room—usually to attend programs in other rooms.

Required programs—those considered essential for enabling students to achieve all forms of literacy, including cultural literacy—are provided in living rooms by hies, but specialized and in-depth courses for college-entry credits are taught elsewhere in the school by teachers called *consultants.* A third category of teachers, called tutors, identify and treat specific learning problems. These skill-centered teachers deal with very small groups or with individuals in lab settings, where they do skill-development and remedial work.

Teachers encourage and *train* children to assume all classroom roles, including teaching roles. To this end, obligatory developmental experiences are thoroughly planned, implemented, and evaluated. Remedial programs are provided for those children whose group-process skills are below the levels required for them to participate fully.

In living rooms, groups of students prepare and present most topics in the required curriculum (which I will describe in more detail later). A team made up of the hi, a paid assistant, and three students is in charge of scheduling activities. By age 13 or 14, the three students will be pretty well capable of running the show, with only occasional consultations with the school staff about changes in or additions to the curriculum.

No matter which living room they are in, individual students continue with their own skills programs (in reading, writing, speaking, listening, ciphering, and so on) and with optional programs (electives for credit). The different treatment of the basic required programs in different living rooms is significant only in terms of process, not in terms of sacred content or academic consequence.

Today, the results of standardized testing are widely misused, especially in the U.S. and Britain and especially with regard to the improper comparison of schools. In the Future School, hies routinely administer tests in the usual areas (e.g., reading, writing, listening, ciphering, cultural literacy), but the results are used only as teaching tools. Even more often, individual students test themselves using computerized tests. Content from any source considered essential for the development of any literacy shows up on such tests and so do content and skills considered cumulative and necessary for programs required later in a student's school career. Tutors and consultants also use standardized tests diagnostically. In addition, consultants use examinations they design themselves that are also part of the "standard evaluation criteria and strategies" specified by the government for each subject.

All hies must be outstanding generalists. The best of them blend a number of disciplines in their required programs and special interests. The borders between traditional subjects are already blurring and eventually will disappear. Instead of being sacred packages of content, school programs will become focal points for explorations that include aspects of many traditional disciplines.

In the Future School those in charge of the living rooms, other full-time faculty members, paid assistants, and even students are required to be on the job seven hours a day, five days a week, 220 days a year.

When we do an about-face and expect all children to become self-propelled learners, each will need high self-esteem and an array of skills. These two characteristics are the fuel of self-propulsion. The specific skills essential to self-propulsion that the schools are responsible for developing are the first order of required programs. These include language literacy (reading, writing, and speaking in all their varied forms); listening; numeracy (including addition, subtraction, division, and elements of mathematics that are essential for everyday life); researching; problem solving; organizing; cultural literacy; and computer literacy.

It is the responsibility of the schools to see that all other activities (save only those bearing on health and student government) are held in abeyance each year until such time as an individual student has reached the expected levels of proficiency in each skill essential to self-propulsion. Programs to develop the skills required for self-propulsion (along with all other required program) must be separate from optional (elective) programs offered for credit. No credit should be given for any required skill development program. In every year of elementary and secondary school, elective programs for credit must be closed to students until they reach the expected level in all required programs.

Another category of required, non-credit programs in which every student must participate every year includes personal fitness (exercise, eating, hygiene, grooming, safety, and drug education), sex education, and student government.

When a student's achievement in these two kinds of required programs has reached the expected level, he or she must also participate every year in a third category of required, noncredit programs, covering such areas of study as international understanding, social service, foreign language, visual and performing arts, children's rights, values (or ethics), current affairs, and media literacy.

A fourth category of required, non-credit programs, equal in status to the third category, are studied at appropriate levels of complexity only at selected ages rather than every year. These include parenting (ages 13 through 18); labor/management relations (ages 6, 11, and 16); law (ages 4, 6, 9, 13, and 16); driving (age 15); science literacy (all ages up to 14); world religions (ages 7, 10, 13, and 16); money and finance (ages 6, 11, and 15); national history (ages 5, 8, 11, and 14); national geography (ages 6, 9, 12, and 15); and job-search and career-planning skills (ages 13, 15, and 17).

Some of the programs in these third and fourth categories will be short units lasting only a few hours, days, or weeks. Others will continue for an entire term or year but will consume only a short time each week. Many programs in all four categories are carried out as living room activities, but others can be assigned to consultants elsewhere in the school.

Students who are achieving at their expected levels in all required programs are allowed to book programs taught by consultants. The electives offered include all the traditional subjects required for college entrance.

As a matter of principle, *Future Schools* are nongraded and tracked only in the sense that all children have the right and responsibility to choose their living rooms and their electives to suit their individual needs. The current model of schooling is not suited to "schooling" children *out of* lower tracks and *into* higher ones. But it is the model of schooling that is wrong, not the concept of tracking.

The way to make students sophisticated in technology is to make the school a technologically rich environment. That most children are not fully computer literate long before the end of elementary school is a stunning indictment of the present model of schooling and of the people who run it. In a revitalized school system in which self-propelled, active learning is the norm, training for computer literacy must include competency testing on every aspect of using the current generation of computers and specific remedial and developmental training for those whose test results indicate need. Every student must have a notebook computer that is compatible with the school's computer, and every student must make routine use of living room camcorders, faxes, copiers, phones, and so on. If we want controlled evolution from the present publicly operated schools to computerized publicly operated schools, every nation must create and fund a comprehensive plan that will phase in these changes.

All changes brought by computers have profound implications, but three of them will shake the foundations of schooling more than anything has since Socrates laid those foundations: unleashed creativity, unlimited access to information, and mastery learning. All of these are gigantic square pegs that won't fit the little round hole of traditional schooling.

The purpose of schooling in the 21st century is to serve all the needs of children that are not met elsewhere in society. Most lower-, middle-, and upper-class parents, even if they are good people, can't provide optimum learning conditions for infants any more than they can for 8- or 12-year-olds. Schools must welcome everyone, from toddlers up to students in their late teens.

Many aspects of the new model are controversial and are likely to remain so. Consider the following prospects.

• Ultimate allegiance will no longer be to just a single nation-state but rather to the planet and to a planetary moral code that students in compulsory global studies programs must synthesize from all cultures on earth.

• It is possible to teach nearly all young people who pass through schools to read, write, speak, and listen. But profound changes in strategy and priorities will have to be made.

• Teachers of media literacy (along with teachers of English) bear primary responsibility for the well-being of democracy through awakening each generation to assaults on freedom of expression and to the consequent obligations of every citizen to maintain and enhance that pivotal freedom.

• National governments should take a great leap toward the universal health of their citizens by supplying two nutritious meals (and vitamin supplements) daily to all children who wish to partake.

• All school sports teams should be organized, managed, coached, and officiated entirely by students, with teachers acting only as consultants. Physical education must be compulsory, and programs must guarantee at least 30 minutes per day of sustained, vigorous exercise for every child.

• For both students and teachers, absenteeism more than 2% of the time should be considered unacceptable.

• Instead of compulsory schooling, we must make universal schooling available and guarantee the right to it. Moreover, the right to schooling must carry with it whatever support is needed to make attendance feasible: fees, supplies, food, clothing, housing, emotional nurturance, and so on.

• There is no other initiative that any developed country could take to reduce the dropout rate and improve attendance that would be nearly as effective as adding residences to schools.

• Teaching should be like other performing arts: the union should negotiate a minimum rate of pay and leave to individuals the decision of whether to work for scale or negotiate payment above scale. Stars command higher pay.

• Even in the present model of schooling, teaching requires organization. In the schools of tomorrow every teacher will need organizational skills on a par with generals and chief executives.

• Responsibility for the formative evaluation of teachers (and hence the routine supervision that is implicit in formative evaluation) must be taken away from principals and given to counselors, who would be employed by every school board to help teachers plan their professional growth.

• Today's curriculum is largely Victorian, a late 19th-century expression of the Industrial Revolution as applied to the education industry. We have tinkered with it, but we have not changed it. To provide promising alternatives—curriculum ideas that will turn schools around and connect them to the present and future instead of the past—we need permanent international, national, and local curriculum think tanks staffed by visionaries.

• If strong nationhood is the goal (rather than a weaker federation of states), the highest level of government must specify the content of each nation's cultural curriculum, because, without a shared national culture and the shared national values that accompany it, successful nationhood is unlikely.

After this article has appeared in the *Kappan*, I expect to receive a number of supportive phone calls. Elation at my end. Will the callers regret that my ideas are too controversial to be discussed at the community level? Disappointment at my end. And 10 years from now, already several years into the new century, will I receive a letter asking whether I know of any place in the U.S. or Canada that has adopted the new model of schooling and childhood? I hope I'll be waiting with a happier answer.